THE NEW NATION
1789–1850

TEACHING GUIDE
FOR THE REVISED 3RD EDITION

OXFORD
UNIVERSITY PRESS

Oxford University Press, Inc., publishes works that
further Oxford University's objective of excellence
in research, scholarship, and education.

Oxford   New York
Auckland   Cape Town   Dar es Salaam   Hong Kong   Karachi
Kuala Lumpur   Madrid   Melbourne   Mexico City   Nairobi
New Delhi   Shanghai   Taipei   Toronto

With offices in
Argentina   Austria   Brazil   Chile   Czech Republic   France   Greece
Guatemala   Hungary   Italy   Japan   Poland   Portugal   Singapore
South Korea   Switzerland   Thailand   Turkey   Ukraine   Vietnam

Writers: Elspeth Leacock, Deborah Parks, Karen Edwards
Editors: Joan Poole, Robert Weisser
Editorial Consultant: Susan Buckley

Published by Oxford University Press, Inc.
198 Madison Avenue, New York, New York, 10016
www.oup.com

ISBN-13: 978-0-19-522305-7 (California edition)   ISBN-13: 978-0-19-518889-9

Project Editor: Matt Fisher
Project Director: Jacqueline A. Ball
Education Consultant: Diane L. Brooks, Ed.D.

Casper Grathwohl, Publisher

Printed in the United States
on acid-free paper

CONTENTS

NOTE FROM THE AUTHOR

Dear Teacher,

It is through story that people have traditionally passed on their ideas, their values, and their heritage. In recent years, however, we have come to think of stories as the property of the youngest of our children. How foolish of us. The rejection of story has made history seem dull. It has turned it into a litany of facts and dates. Stories make the past understandable (as well as enjoyable). Stories tell us who we are and where we've been. Without knowledge of our past, we can't make sense of the present.

As a former teacher, I knew of the need for a narrative history for young people, so I sat down and wrote one. (It took me seven years.) I was tired of seeing children struggle with arm-breaking, expensive books. I wanted my books to be inexpensive, light in weight, and user-friendly. Thanks to creative partnering by American Historical Publications and Oxford University Press, that's the way they are.

Called *A History of US*, mine is a set of 11 books. My hope is that they will help make American history—our story—a favorite subject again. It is important that it be so. As we prepare for the 21st century, we are becoming an increasingly diverse people. While we need to celebrate and enjoy that diversity, we also need to find solid ground to stand on together. Our history can provide that commonality. We are a nation built on ideas, on great documents, on individual achievement—and none of that is the property of any one group of us. Harriet Tubman, Abraham Lincoln, Emily Dickinson, Sequoya, and Duke Ellington belong to all of us—and so do our horse thieves, slave owners, and robber barons. We need to consider them all.

Now, to be specific, what do I intend these books to do in your classrooms? First of all, I want to help turn your students into avid readers. I want them to understand that nonfiction can be as exciting as fiction. (Besides, it is the kind of reading they'll meet most in the adult world.) I want to stretch their minds. I've written stories, but the stories are true stories. In nonfiction you grapple with the real world. I want to help children understand how fascinating that process can be.

I've tried to design books that I would have liked as a teacher—books that are flexible, easy-to-read, challenging, and idea-centered, that will lead children into energetic discussions. History can do that. It involves issues we still argue about. It gives us material with which to make judgments. It allows for comparisons. It hones the mind.

People all over this globe are dying—literally—because they want to live under a democracy. We've got the world's model and most of us don't understand or appreciate it. I want to help children learn about their country so they will be intelligent citizens. I want them to understand the heritage that they share with all the diverse people who are us—the citizens of the United States.

For some of your students, these books may be an introduction to history. What they actually remember will be up to you. Books can inspire and excite, but understanding big ideas and remembering details takes some reinforced learning. You'll find many suggestions for that in this Teaching Guide.

What you do with *A History of Us* and this Teaching Guide will depend, of course, on you and your class. You may have students read every chapter or only some chapters, many volumes or only a few. (But, naturally, I hope they'll read it all. Our history makes good reading.) I hope you'll use the books to teach reading and thinking skills as well as history and geography. We need to stop thinking of subjects as separate from each other. We talk about integrating the curriculum; we need to really do it. History, broadly, is the story of a culture—and that embraces art, music, science, mathematics, and literature. (You'll find some of all of those in these books.)

Reading *A History of Us* is easy; even young children seem to enjoy it. But some of the concepts in the books are not easy. They can be challenging to adults, which means that the volumes can be read on several levels. The idea is to get students excited by history and stretched mentally—at whatever their level of understanding. (Don't worry if every student doesn't understand every word. We adults don't expect that of our reading; we should allow for the same variety of comprehension among student readers.)

This Teaching Guide is filled with ideas meant to take the students back to the text to do a careful, searching read. It will also send them out to do research and writing and discovering on their own. The more you involve your students, the more they will understand and retain. Confucius, one of the worlds' great teachers, had this to say:

Tell me and I will forget. Show me and I will remember. Involve me and I will understand.

Joy Hakim with two of her favorite readers, her grandchildren, Natalie and Sam Johnson

History is about discovering. It is a voyage that you and your students can embark on together. I wish you good sailing.

Joy Hakim

I. STUDENT EDITION

- By Joy Hakim, winner of James Michener Prize in Writing
- Engaging, friendly narrative
- A wide range of primary sources in every chapter
- Period illustrations and specially commissioned maps
- New atlas section customized for each book

II. TEACHING GUIDE

- Standards-based instruction
- Wide range of activities and classroom approaches
- Strategies for universal access and improving literacy (ELL, struggling readers, advanced learners)
- Multiple assessment tools

III. STUDENT STUDY GUIDE

- Exercises correlated to Student Edition and Teaching Guide
- Portfolio approach
- Activities for every level of learning
- Literacy through reading and writing
- Completely new for 2005

SOURCEBOOK AND INDEX

- Broad selection of primary sources in each subject area
- Ideal resource for in-class exercises and unit projects

Each Teaching Guide is organized into Parts. Each Part includes Chapter Lessons, a Team Learning Project from Johns Hopkins University, Check-up Tests, and other assessments and activities

PARTS
Unify chapter lessons with themes and projects.

INTRODUCTION
▶ Lists standards addressed in each chapter
▶ Gives objectives and big ideas and suggests projects and lessons to set context for the chapters

SUMMARY
▶ Gives assessment ideas and debate, ethics, and interdisciplinary project ideas

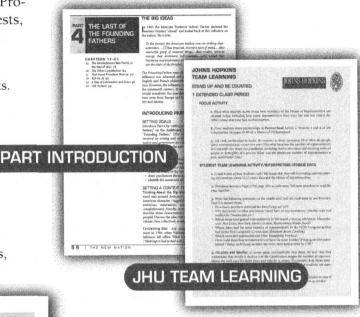

PART INTRODUCTION

JHU TEAM LEARNING

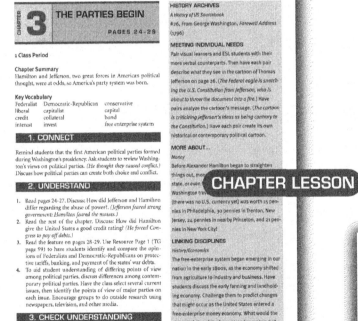

CHAPTER LESSON

JHU TEAM LEARNING
▶ Each Part contains a cooperative learning project developed by the Talent Development Middle School Program at Johns Hopkins University specifically for *A History of US*.

CHAPTER LESSONS
▶ Correlated to the new Student Study Guide
▶ Ideas for enrichment, discussion, writing, vocabulary, and projects

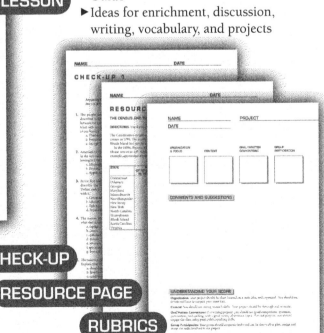

RUBRICS, CHECK-UPS, AND RESOURCE PAGES
▶ Reproduce and hand out for assessment and activities

CHECK-UP

RESOURCE PAGE

RUBRICS

PLANNING LESSONS USING TEACHING AND STUDENT STUDY GUIDES

SET A CONTEXT FOR READING

The books in *A History of US* are written so that a student can read them from cover to cover. You can strengthen students' connection to major themes through introductory lessons or projects. These lessons can be found in the introduction to the Teaching Guide and the opening pages for each Part.

Some students, especially developing readers or those learning English as a second language, may need extra help building background knowledge before reading the text. For these students, exercises in the Teaching and Student Study Guides help to set a context for reading. Look for **Connect** (in the Teaching Guide) and **Access** (in the Student Study Guide) sections. Also, refer to the Improving Literacy section (pages 20–25) for general strategies from an expert.

CREATE A FLEXIBLE CLASSROOM PLAN USING THE STUDENT STUDY GUIDE AND TEACHING GUIDE

The ancillary materials for *A History of US* have been developed for multiple teaching strategies, depending on the particular needs and abilities of your students. Choose an approach that works best for your students. Here are a few options:

▶ **Assign Student Study Guide activities as best suits your class needs**
The Student Study Guide activities are designed to reinforce and clarify content. They were created for students to complete with a minimum of explanation or supervision. The Student Study Guide can be used as homework or in class. The activities can be assigned concurrently with the reading, to help comprehend the material and come to class ready for in-depth discussion of the reading, or as a follow-up to the reading.

▶ **Use Teaching Guide activities to build and enrich comprehension**
The activities from the **Understand** section of each Chapter Lesson, as well as the sidebars, are meant to foster a dynamic, active, vocal classroom. They center on participatory small group and partner projects and focused individual work.

▶ **Use group projects to broaden understanding**
Other suggestions for group projects are found throughout the Teaching Guide, in Part Openers, Part Summaries, and Chapter Lessons. These activities cover a variety of content standard-related topics.

Also, developed specially for *A History of US* are the Johns Hopkins Team Learning Activities, which correlate to Part-wide themes and use cooperative learning models developed by Johns Hopkins University's Talent Development Middle School Program. (For more on these activities and how to use them, see page 21.) Also published by Oxford University Press, a complete curriculum, based on Team Learning Activities for *A History of US* is available. For more information, log on to *www.oup.com*.

Whether projects and assignments are geared toward solidifying understanding of the text or enriching connections with other disciplines is up to you.

▶ **Assign individual work**
Many exercises from the Teaching Guide **Check Understanding** section can be used for individual homework assignments. Student Study Guide pages can be assigned for homework as well.

► **Encourage students to create history journals for a portfolio approach**
Student Study Guide pages can be removed from the book and kept in a binder with writing assignments, artwork, and notes from projects as an individual portfolio. This approach creates a history journal, which has many benefits. It can be worked on at home and brought into class for assessment or sharing. It is a student's very own journal, where personal creativity can find an outlet. It also keeps all work organized and in order. Both the Teaching Guide and Student Study Guide contain a variety of analytical and creative writing projects that can be addressed in the history journal.

► **Assess however and whenever you need to**
This Teaching Guide contains the following assessment tools: cumulative, synthesis-based project ideas at the end of each Part, wrap-up tests, and scoring rubrics.

RUBRICS

At the back of this Teaching Guide you will find four reproducible rubric pages.

1. The Scoring Rubric page explains the evaluation categories. You may wish to go over and discuss each of these categories and points with your students.

2. A shortened handout version of the Scoring Rubric page has been included, with explanations of the categories and room for comments.

3. A student self-scoring rubric has been included. Use it to prompt your students to describe and evaluate both their work and participation in group projects.

4. A library/media center research log has also been included. Use this rubric as an aid to student research. It will help them plan and brainstorm research methods, record results, and evaluate their sources.

ASSESSMENT OPPORTUNITIES

Part Summaries were written specifically to give assessment ideas. They do this in two ways:

1. They refer to Part Check-Ups—reproducible tests at the back of the Teaching Guide that combine multiple choice, short answer, and an essay question to present a comprehensive assessment that covers the chapters in each Part.

2. They contains additional essay questions for alternate assessment as well as numerous project ideas. Projects can be assessed using the scoring rubrics at the back of the Teaching Guide.

ANSWER KEYS

An answer key at the back of the Teaching Guide contains answers for Part Check-Ups, Resource Pages, and Student Study Guide activities.

The Student Study Guide complements the activities in the Teaching Guide with exercises that build a context for the reading and strengthen analysis skills. Many activities encourage informal small group or family participation. In addition, the following features make it an effective teaching tool:

FLEXIBILITY

You can use the Study Guide in the classroom, with individuals or small groups, or send it home for homework. You can distribute the entire guide to students; however, the pages are perforated so you can remove and distribute only the pertinent lessons.

A page on reports and special projects in the front of the Study Guide directs students to the "More Books to Read" resource in the student edition. This feature gives students general guidance on doing research and devising independent study projects of their own.

FACSIMILE SPREAD

The Study Guide begins with a facsimile spread from the Student Edition. This spread gives reading strategies and highlights key features: captions, primary sources, sidebars, headings, etymologies. The spread supplies the contextualization students need to fully understand the material.

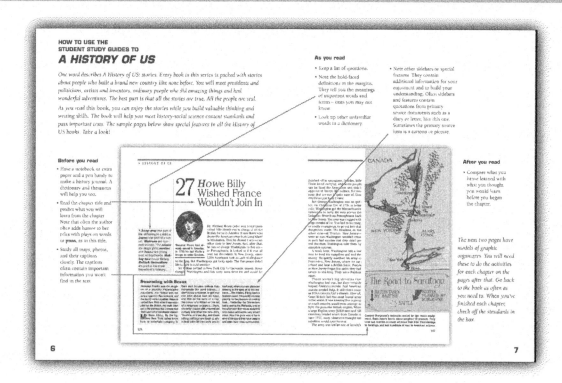

PORTFOLIO APPROACH

The Study Guide pages are three-hole-punched so they can be integrated with notebook paper in a looseleaf binder. This history journal or portfolio can become both a record of content mastery and an outlet for each student's unique creative expression. Responding to prompts, students can write poetry or songs, plays and character sketches, create storyboards or cartoons, or construct multi-layered timelines.

The portfolio approach gives students unlimited opportunities for practice in areas that need strengthening. And the Study Guide pages in the portfolio make a valuable assessment tool for you. It is an ongoing record of performance that can be reviewed and graded periodically.

GRAPHIC ORGANIZERS

This feature contains reduced models of seven graphic organizers referenced frequently in the guide. Using these devices will help students organize the material so it is more accessible. (Full-size reproducibles of each graphic organizer are provided at the back of this Teaching Guide.) These graphic organizers include: outline, main idea map, K-W-L chart (What I Know, What I Want to Know, What I Learned), Venn diagram, timeline, sequence of events chart, and t-chart.

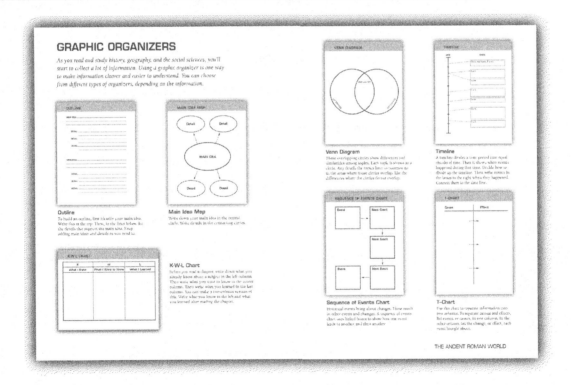

Each chapter lesson is designed to draw students into the subject matter. Recurring features and exercises challenge their knowledge and allow them to practice valuable analysis skills. Activities in the Teaching Guide and Student Study Guide complement but do not duplicate each other. Together they offer a wide range of class work, group projects, and opportunities for further study and assessment that can be tailored to all ability levels.

CHAPTER SUMMARY
briefly reviews big ideas from the chapter.

ACCESS
makes content accessible to students of all levels by incorporating graphic organizers into note taking.

WRITING
gives students writing suggestions drawn from the material. A writing assignment may stem from a vocabulary word, a historical event, a person, or a reading of a primary source. The assignment can take any number of forms: newspaper article, letter, short essay, a scene with dialogue, a diary entry.

CHAPTER 2 — ABOUT BEING A PRESIDENT

SUMMARY *George Washington chose advisers to help him run the country.*

ACCESS

Have you ever tried to do a really hard job by yourself? Hard jobs are usually easier when you get people to help. President Washington could not run the country by himself. He needed advisers to assist him. Copy the main idea map from page 8 into your history journal. In the largest circle, put Washington's name. In each of the smaller circles, write the name of one of the people who helped Washington govern the nation. Below each name, write the job that the person had.

WORD BANK   precedent   executive   legislative   judicial   cabinet   dictatorship

Choose words from the word bank to complete the sentences. One word is not used at all.

1. The _____ branch includes the nation's courts.

2. A government that is run by an all-powerful leader is called a _____.

3. The president is the head of the _____ branch.

4. Washington chose Henry Knox to serve in his _____.

5. Congress is also called the _____ branch.

WORD PLAY

In the dictionary, look up the word you did not use. Write a sentence using that word.

WITH A PARENT OR PARTNER

The United States has a three-branch government. Write the name of each branch at the top of a piece of paper. Below each name, write five words that relate to that particular branch of government. Ask a parent or partner to do the same. Then read your lists to each other.

WORKING WITH PRIMARY SOURCES

In 1792 Dr. Benjamin Rush wrote this about a hot air balloon flight by Jean-Pierre François Blanchard:

> For some time days past the conversation in our city has turned wholly upon Mr. Blanchard's late Aerial Voyage. It was truly a sublime sight. Every faculty of the mind was seized, expanded and captivated by it, 40,000 people concentrating their eyes and thoughts at the same instant, upon the same object, and all deriving nearly the same degree of pleasure from it.

1. How did Benjamin Rush feel about Blanchard's flight?

2. How did the people of Philadelphia feel about Blanchard's flight?

WRITING

Imagine that you are in Philadelphia watching Blanchard's flight. In your history journal, write a letter to a friend describing the event in your own words.

12   CHAPTER 2

CHAPTER 3

THE PARTIES BEGIN

SUMMARY *Alexander Hamilton and Thomas Jefferson had different ideas about what was best for the country. Their disagreements led to America's first party system.*

ACCESS

What is a political party? How many political parties can you think of? When George Washington took office, the United States did not have any political parties. He thought they caused conflict. Copy the main idea map from page 8 into your history journal. In the largest circle, put *Hamilton and Jefferson's Disagreements.* As you read the chapter, write an issue they disagreed about in each of the smaller circles.

WORD BANK

Federalist   liberal   credit   interest   Democratic-Republican   capitalist   collateral   invest   conservative   capital   bond   free enterprise system

Choose words from the word bank to complete the sentences. One word is not used at all.

1. Thomas Jefferson was the leader of the _____ party.

2. If you borrow money, you must pay _____.

3. A capitalist system is sometimes called a _____.

4. A _____ favors civil liberties, democratic reforms and the use of governmental power to promote social progress.

5. The _____ party consisted of Alexander Hamilton's supporters.

6. When people get a loan, sometimes they must provide _____.

7. A _____ is a written promise to pay back a loan.

8. Many farmers and solders decided to _____ in the new U.S. government.

9. A _____ is someone who is reluctant to make changes.

10. Another word for borrowing power is _____.

11. _____ is money, or any goods or assets that can be turned into money.

WORD PLAY

Identify two of the above terms that have similar meanings. Next identify two of the above terms that have opposite meanings. Write your answers below.

_____

CRITICAL THINKING   COMPARE AND CONTRAST

The phrases below describe Alexander Hamilton and Thomas Jefferson. In your history journal, copy the Venn Diagram on page 9. Write *Hamilton* above one circle and *Jefferson* above the other circle. The phrases that apply to only one person go in that person's circle. The phrases that apply to both go in the area where the two circles connect.

wanted a free education amendment

concerned about balancing liberty and power

wanted the government to pay off its debt

wanted aristocratic leaders to govern

had faith in ordinary people

feared the masses

headed a major political party

feared a powerful government

fought for freedom of the press

encouraged business and industry

WORKING WITH PRIMARY SOURCES

Stephen Vincent Benét wrote a poem about one of the Founding Fathers.

He could handle the Nation's dollars
With a magic that's known to few,
He could talk with the wits and scholars

And scratch like a wildcat, too.
And he yoked the States together
With a yoke that is strong and stout.

Who is the subject of the poem? Which lines reveal the person's identity? Circle your answers in the poem.

THE NEW NATION   **13**

Strategic Methods for Content Learning

READING HISTORY

A PRACTICAL GUIDE TO IMPROVING LITERACY

JANET ALLEN
with Christine Landaker

Enhancing reading skills and learning history are inextricably linked. Students for whom reading is a challenge have difficulty immersing themselves in books and in historical narratives. With these students, improving literacy becomes crucial for teaching history.

Especially with struggling readers and English-language learners, comprehending the text is the first (and often most difficult) step toward engaging the story. *Reading History: A Practical Guide to Improving Literacy*, by Dr. Janet Allen, was written specifically to address teaching history to these students. *Reading History* is a book of instructional strategies for "building meaningful background knowledge that will support reading, writing, and research."

The instructional strategies in *Reading History* are modular components that can be understood with a minimum of instruction and can be applied easily as pre- and post-reading and writing activities. The Wordstorming and List-Group-Label exercises below are two examples of the simple and effective activities that can be the difference between giving information and building background that helps to improve literacy.

Dr. Allen and colleague Christine Landaker used *A History of US* to help create and illustrate the activities in *Reading History*, and examples from *A History of US* appear throughout the book, dovetailing the two books into a single, comprehensive, and successful literacy-based History curriculum.

From Reading History

WORDSTORMING

1. Ask students to write down all the words they can think of related to a given word (concept, theme, target word).

2. When students have exhausted their contributions, help them add to their individual lists by giving some specific directions.
   Can you think of words that describe someone without _____?
   Can you think of words that would show what someone might see, hear, feel, touch, smell in a situation filled with _____?

3. Ask students to group and label their words.

4. Add any words you think should be included and ask students to put them in the right group.

LIST-GROUP-LABEL

1. List all of the words you can think of related to _____ (major concept of text).

2. Group words that you have listed by words that have something in common.

3. Once words are grouped, decide on a label for each group.

USING THE JOHNS HOPKINS TEAM LEARNING ACTIVITIES

JOHNS HOPKINS
U N I V E R S I T Y

The Talent Development Middle School Program at Johns Hopkins University is a project of the Center for the Social Organization of Schools (CSOS). *A History of US* is the core of the American history curriculum in this whole-school reform effort. Oxford University Press proudly includes in this Teaching Guide selected lessons developed by Susan Dangel and Maria Gariott at the Talent Development Middle School Program.

You will find one Johns Hopkins Team Learning Activity at the end of each Part in this Teaching Guide. Keyed to appropriate chapters, the Team Learning Activity provides an opportunity to use cooperative learning models based on *A History of US*.

Each Activity begins with a Focus Activity that introduces the lesson, engages students, and draws on students' prior knowledge.

The heart of the lesson is a Team Learning Activity. In teams, students investigate lesson content, solve problems, use information for a purpose, and apply the tools of the historian.

Within the Student Team Learning Activity, the following techniques and strategies may be employed:

▶ Brainstorming: Students generate as many ideas as possible within a set time, before discussing and evaluating them.

▶ Roundtable: A brainstorming technique in which each team member contributes ideas on one sheet of paper and passes it to the next student. In Simultaneous Roundtable, more than one sheet is passed at the same time.

▶ Round Robin: An oral form of brainstorming in which one team member at a time states an idea.

▶ Think-Pair-Share: Students think about content or consider a question, then share their responses with a partner. In Think-Team-Share, students think through the prompt on their own and then share as a team.

▶ Partner Read: Students share a reading assignment with a partner.

▶ Timed Telling: A student or team is given a fixed time to share information, opinions, or results with the class.

▶ Team Investigation: Working in teams, students search and analyze the text, primary source materials, or other resource materials; draw conclusions; and make connections.

▶ Jigsaw: Within each team, students select or are assigned specific questions or subjects on which to become experts. Experts meet and investigate in Expert Teams, then regroup in their original teams to report out their findings.

▶ Numbered Heads: Each team member is assigned a number—1, 2, 3, and so on. Team members work together on the team learning activity. The teacher selects one number and asks the person with that number in each team to report the team response.

PROVIDING ACCESS

The books in this series are written in a lively, narrative style to inspire a love of reading. English language learners and struggling readers are given special consideration within the program's exercises and activities. And students who love to read and learn will also benefit from the program's rich and varied material. Following are expert strategies to make sure each and every student gets the most out of the subjects you will teach through *A History of US*.

ADVANCED LEARNERS

Every classroom has students who finish the required assignments and then want additional challenges. Fortunately, the very nature of history and social science offers a wide range of opportunities for students to explore topics in greater depth. Encourage them to come up with their own ideas for an additional assignment. Determine the final product, its presentation, and a timeline for completion.

Research

Students can develop in-depth understanding through seeking information, exploring ideas, asking and answering questions, making judgments, considering points of view, and evaluating actions and events. They will need access to a wide range of resource materials: the Internet, maps, encyclopedias, trade books, magazines, dictionaries, artifacts, newspapers, museum catalogues, brochures, and the library. See the "More Books to Read" section at the end of the Student Edition for good jumping-off points.

Projects

You can encourage students to capitalize on their strengths as learners (visual, verbal, kinesthetic, or musical) or to try a new way of responding. Students can prepare a debate or write a persuasive paper, play, skit, poem, song, dance, game, puzzle, or biography. They can create an alphabet book on the topic, film a video, do a book talk, or illustrate a book. They can render charts, graphs, or other visual representations. Allow for creativity and support students' thinking.

ENGLISH LANGUAGE LEARNERS

For English learners to achieve academic success, the instructional considerations for teachers include two mandates:

▶ Help them attain grade level, content area knowledge, and academic language.
▶ Provide for the development of English language proficiency.

To accomplish these goals, you should plan lessons that reflect the student's level of English proficiency. Students progress through five developmental levels as they increase in language proficiency:

▶ Beginning and Early Intermediate (grade level material will be mostly incomprehensible, students need a great deal of teacher support)
▶ Intermediate (grade level work will be a challenge)
▶ Early Advanced and Advanced (close to grade level reading and writing, students continue to need support)

Tap Prior Knowledge

What students know about the topic will help determine your next steps for instruction. Using K-W-L charts, brainstorming, and making lists are ways to find out what they know. English learners bring a rich cultural diversity into the classroom. By sharing what they know, students can connect their knowledge and experiences to the course.

Set the Context

Use different tools to make new information understandable. These can be images, artifacts, maps, timelines, illustrations, charts, videos, or graphic organizers. Techniques such as role-playing and story-boarding can also be helpful. Speak in shorter sentences, with careful enunciation, expanded explanations, repetitions, and paraphrasing. Use fewer idiomatic expressions.

Show—Don't Just Tell

English learners often get lost as they listen to directions, explanations, lectures, and discussions. By showing students what is expected, you can help them participate more fully in classroom activities. Students need to be shown how to use the graphic organizers in the student study guide, as well as other blackline masters for note-taking and practice. An overhead transparency with whole or small groups is also effective.

Use the Text

Because of unfamiliar words, students will need help with understanding. Teach them to preview the chapter using text features (headings, bold print, sidebars, italics). See the suggestions in the facsimile of the Student Edition, shown on pages 6–7 of the Student Study Guide. Show students organizing structures such as cause and effect or comparing and contrasting. Have students read to each other in pairs. Help them create word banks, charts, and graphic organizers. Discuss the main idea after reading.

Check for Understanding

Rather than simply ask students if they understand, stop frequently and ask them to paraphrase or expand on what you just said. Such techniques will give you a much clearer assessment of their understanding.

Provide for Interaction

As students interact with the information and speak their thoughts, their content knowledge and academic language skills improve. Increase interaction in the classroom through cooperative learning, small group work, and partner share. By working and talking with others, students can practice asking and answering questions.

Use Appropriate Assessment

When modifying the instruction, you will also need to modify the assessment. Multiple choice, true and false, and other criterion reference tests are suitable, but consider changing test format and structure. English learners are constantly improving their language proficiency in their oral and written responses, but they are often grammatically incorrect. Remember to be thoughtful and fair about giving students credit for their content knowledge and use of academic language, even if their English isn't perfect.

IMPROVING LITERACY WITH A HISTORY OF US

STRUGGLING READERS

Some students struggle to understand the information presented in a textbook. The following strategies for content-area reading can help students improve their ability to make comparisons, sequence events, determine importance, summarize, evaluate, synthesize, analyze, and solve problems.

Build Knowledge of Genre

Both fiction and narrative nonfiction genres are incorporated into *A History of US*. This combination of genres makes the text interesting and engaging. But teachers must be sure students can identify and use the organizational structures of both genres.

The textbook has a wealth of the text features of nonfiction: bold and italic print, sidebars, headings and subheadings, labels, captions, and "signal words" such as first, next, and finally. Teaching these organizational structures and text features is essential for struggling readers.

Fiction

Each chapter is a story

Setting: historical time and place

Characters: historical figures

Plot: problems, roadblocks, and resolutions

Non-Fiction

Content: historical information

Organizational structure: cause/effect, sequence of events, problem/solution

Other features: maps, timelines, sidebars, photographs, primary sources

Build Background

Having background information about a topic makes reading about it so much easier. When students lack background information, teachers can preteach or "front load" concepts and vocabulary, using a variety of instructional techniques. Conduct a "chapter or bookwalk," looking at titles, headings, and other text features to develop a big picture of the content. Focus in new vocabulary words during the "walk" and create a word bank with illustrations for future reference. Read aloud key passages and discuss the meaning. Focus on the timeline and maps to help students develop a sense of time and place. Show a video, go to a website, and have trade books and magazines on the topic available for student exploration.

Comprehension Strategies

While reading, successful readers are predicting, making connections, monitoring, visualizing, questioning, inferring, and summarizing. Struggling readers have a harder time with these "in the head" processes. The following strategies will help these students construct meaning from the text until they are able to do it on their own.

Predict

Before reading, conduct a picture and text feature "tour" of the chapter to make predictions. Ask students if they remember if this has ever happened before, to predict what might happen this time.

Make Connections

Help students relate content to their background (text to text, text to self, and text to the world).

Monitor And Confirm

Encourage students to stop reading when they come across an unknown word, phrase, or concept. In their notebooks, have them make a note of text they don't understand and ask for clarification or figure it out. While this activity slows down reading at first, it is effective in improving skills over time.

Visualize

Students benefit from imagining the events described in a story. Sketching scenes, story-boarding, role-playing, and looking for sensory details all help students with this strategy.

Infer

Help students look beyond the literal meaning of a text to understand deeper meanings. Graphic organizers and discussions provide opportunities to broaden their understanding. Looking closely at the "why" of historical events helps students infer.

Question And Discuss

Have students jot down their questions as they read, and then share them during discussions. Or have students come up with the type of questions they think a teacher would ask. Over time students will develop more complex inferential questions, which lead to group discussions. Questioning and discussing also helps students see ideas from multiple perspectives and draw conclusions, both critical skills for understanding history.

Determine Importance

Teach students how to decide what is most important from all the facts and details in nonfiction. After reading for an overall understanding, they can go back to highlight important ideas, words, and phrases. Clues for determining importance include bold or italic print, signal words, and other text features. A graphic organizer such as a main idea map also helps.

Teach and Practice Decoding Strategies

Rather than simply defining an unfamiliar word, teach struggling readers decoding strategies: have them look at the prefix, suffix, and root to help figure out the new word, look for words they know within the word, use the context for clues, and read further or reread.

— Cheryl A. Caldera, M.A.
Literacy Coach

TEACHING STRATEGIES FOR *THE NEW NATION*

INTRODUCING BOOK FOUR

We the People of the United States, in Order to form a more perfect Union, establish Justice, insure domestic Tranquillity, provide for the common defense, promote the general Welfare, and secure the Blessings of Liberty to ourselves and our Posterity, do ordain and establish this CONSTITUTION for the United States of America.

HISTORICAL OVERVIEW

Thus reads the preamble to the Constitution, written in 1787. This document created both a nation of united states and a democratic form of governing. These two great issues—union and democracy—would remain the focal point of great passions for decades to come and would eventually lead to the nation's greatest trial in the Civil War.

What was the source of these issues? The struggle for union arose out of the obvious failure of the Articles of Confederation. Even the most ardent states' rights champion was convinced that a stronger federal government of some sort was needed for the nation to maintain its independence and to prevent civil war. The conflict over federal versus state powers would continue, however, and does so to this day.

The roots of America's democracy are more elusive. A look at the colonial experience reveals love of monarchy and hierarchy. All of the royal family's birthdays were faithfully observed, and the king was blessed on a regular basis by everyone. English manners were mimicked no matter how inappropriate they were to their communities. And it was generally accepted that "commoners," or "simple people," would defer to their superiors, the "gentle people," in matters of public policy. John Randolph declared in 1774, "When I mention the public, I mean to include only the rational part of it, the ignorant vulgar are…unable to manage the reins of government."

But America was not England, and the roots of American democracy can be discovered when the soil is scratched. The society was more mobile than that of the old country. Power and position were open to more white men in the United States than anywhere else in the world. (Women, African-Americans, and Native Americans did not enjoy this advantage.) The Peter Zenger trial established freedom of the press. Cheap land attracted small farmers to the West where life was independent and free, and in the East, town meetings provided for some democratic experiences. And Native Americans, with their more egalitarian societies, were an inspiration to some.

The taproot of American democracy may be found in the Revolution itself, in the political opportunity it created. Once English authority was overthrown, there were few undemocratic social structures to be destroyed. As the French writer Alexis de Tocqueville observed, the American "arrived at a state of democracy without having to endure a democratic revolution,…he is born free without having to become so."

There were no feudal obstructions to hamper the Founding Fathers. There were also no enemies threatening invasion. The Atlantic Ocean protected the nation from potentially threatening armies, leaving the young nation able to concentrate on development, rather than defense.

Inauguration of George Washington

Meriwether Lewis and William Clark

Battle of Tippecanoe

Inauguration of Andrew Jackson

The final factor was the time period itself. In Europe, Enlightenment scholars were questioning governments, freedom, and power. They were reexamining Greek and Roman political ideas. When Americans looked to Europe for inspiration, they found hundreds of books, lectures, papers and many wonderful ideas just waiting to be tested.

Relative security, few established social structures, a little democratic experience, seemingly endless land and resources, new independence, heads full of ideas—these were the ingredients in 1789 available to the young nation as it stood on the brink of a transformation that would touch every aspect of society. An extraordinary growth of the economy, of the land, and of the population would dramatically alter lives and landscape. The pace, the scope, and the cost of these transformations can be heard in the voices of contemporaries.

Three or four thousand soldiers drive the wandering native tribes before them; behind the armed men woodcutters advance, penetrating the forests, scaring off the wild beasts, exploring the course of rivers, and preparing the triumphal progress of civilization across the wilderness.

At present all is energy and enterprise; everything is in a state of transition, but of rapid improvement—so rapid, indeed, that those who would describe America now would have to correct all in the short space of ten years; for ten years in America is almost equal to a century in the old continent.

As observed in these diaries, the unprecedented pace and immeasurable scope of change had its cost in conflict. As opportunity lured settlers west, Native American homelands were lost forever. When the federal government developed and grew powerful, the states were threatened. When the cotton empire spanned the South, the fate of generations of black Americans was sealed. When northern industry developed, strife and waste followed closely behind. Alongside growth, conflicts grew apace. But conflict did not scare Americans in that prewar era. Their plans and their actions were bold.

By 1848, the United States was so transformed physically, politically, economically, and culturally, that it bore little resemblance to the union that in 1787 embarked upon the great democratic experiment filled with confidence and optimism, fears and passion. The stories of the men and women who steered the course, who rode in steerage or in bondage, and those whose lives and lands were overwhelmed in these times form the stories of Book Four.

Slaves being transported in shackles

INTRODUCING THE BIG IDEAS

Power, **growth**, and **identity** are the Big Ideas of *The New Nation* (Book Four of *A History of US*). Introducing your students to these concepts at the beginning will help them put together the pieces of the puzzle to make sense of the past.

Word Webs   Write on the chalkboard the title of this book, *The New Nation*. Ask students to define what makes a nation new. How might a new nation differ from an older, more established one? Then write *power* on the chalkboard, and work with students to create a word web for this word. Help students to link the concept of power with new nations. Ask: How would a new nation's concerns with power differ from those of a more established nation?

Create another word web around the word *growth*. Two important words to include are *expansion* and *development*. America was about to embark on a period of great expansion and development. Students might compare the nation's growth with their own experience. They are growing larger, but they are also developing. The United States would develop a national character, an economy, a foreign policy, as well as a new political system. Spatially, the nation would double its original size.

For Discussion   Point out that all this growth changes a nation's identity, just as students' own identities change as they grow up. You might also ask students to describe the identities or characteristics of different regions of the United States today. Are they all the same? Remind them of the historical differences in the regions of colonial America (New England, Middle Colonies, Southern Colonies, frontier). Ask students to speculate about how regional identities may differ as the nation develops. (*Students should be aware of how developments in mass communication and transportation affect regional identities.*)

FOCUSING ON LITERACY
SETTING THE CONTEXT

The World Turned Upside Down   Set the context for reading this volume by reading aloud the words of the song "The World Turn'd Upside Down." This tune was played by the British as they lay down their arms at Yorktown, ending the War of Independence.

If the buttercups buzzed after the bee,
If boats were on land, churches on sea,
If ponies rode men, and if grass ate the cows,
And cats should be chased into holes by the mouse;
If the mamas sold their babies to gypsies for half a crown,
If summer were spring, and the other way 'round,
Then all the world would be upside down.

Ask students to imagine the feelings of the soldiers of the most powerful nation on earth as they surrendered. (*disbelief, denial,* and so on) Then ask them to consider how the Americans must have felt. (*self-confident and optimistic*)

INTRODUCING THE BOOK WITH PROJECTS AND ACTIVITIES

USING THE RUBRICS

To assess these writing assignments, group projects, and activities, scoring rubrics have been provided at the back to this Teaching Guide. Be sure to explain the rubrics to your students.

Setting the Stage   Explain that with these feelings and a plan, Americans bravely struck out to make their new nation work. Tell students that Book Four spans six decades, from 1789 to about 1850. To help students understand the concept of a sixty-year period, explain that if a person were born in 1789 and lived until 1850, he or she would be roughly the age of a grandparent. Tell students that the book opens with the story of the nation's beginning in the early spring of 1789 when George Washington was the first to be elected to the office of president of the United States. The book ends with the story of the great debate in Congress over an issue that threatened the nation's very existence. The years between these events were packed with power struggles, expansion, and the creation of a distinct national identity

To set the stage for Book Four, have students read the Preface on pages 9-12. Help students envision life in your own community at the opening of the nineteenth century. (You may want to assign students to investigate this further with local and state historical societies.)

Bill of Rights   Before students begin Chapter 1, you may also wish to have them review the Bill of Rights. Ask ten students each to summarize one of the ten rights and explain its importance.

MAKING JUDGMENTS

Making judgments is an important skill that students will exercise frequently as they read and respond to Book Four. Students' judgments should be based on their own experiences and values and on historical evidence.

Teaching suggestions ask students to make judgments about why the nation divided into distinct regions over the issues of slavery, Native American lands, states' rights, and political parties.

Joy Hakim begins the book with the question "How can a nation built on the idea that 'all men are created equal' keep some people in chains?" This and other questions raised by Book Four are hard for students to answer. In order to respond with a clear judgment, students must compare and contrast regions and evaluate the causes and effects behind such a paradox.

Venn Diagrams   Use various graphic organizers to help students amass the information they need to make clear, well-formulated judgments. For example, students can create large Venn diagrams to compare and contrast the three key regions in the developing nation: North, South, and West. This will help them understand the important role played by regional differences.

Cause and Effect Charts   To enable students to understand why the economies of the North and South evolved the way they did, students can create cause-and-effect chains and charts. When students do formulate a judgment, they can use a chart with these headings: *Question, Evidence from Text, Evidence from My Own Experience, Judgment.*

READING FURTHER

Biography Library Ask students to bring in biographies of the many people who helped form a brand-new people called *Americans*:

- political leaders such as George Washington, John Adams, Thomas Jefferson, and Andrew Jackson
- girls who worked in the nation's first mills, such as Lucy Larcom
- African-Americans who fought for freedom, such as Frederick Douglass
- explorers, such as Lewis and Clark
- inventors who changed how people in America lived, such as Robert Fulton and Eli Whitney
- Native Americans who struggled to protect a way of life, such as Osceola, Tecumseh, and Red Jacket

ONGOING PROJECTS

The following activities bridge the seven parts in *The New Nation*.

USING TIME LINES

Author Joy Hakim advises that a sense of chronology—rather than memorized dates—is what matters for students. Various kinds of time lines are invaluable aids in building this understanding of historical sequence.

The author helps set a framework in time by providing a Chronology at the end of each of the ten books in this series. A class time line, started at the beginning of the year, will help students place each segment of their study in sequence. You and your students may create such a time line with long sheets of butcher paper. Connected sheets of computer paper, calculator paper, or a clothesline also work well. Invite the class to illustrate the time line with drawings, maps, and photocopied illustrations.

When appropriate, you may want to help students design a means of portraying eras on their time lines, For example, the Federalist, Jeffersonian, and Jacksonian eras are part of Book Four. Horizontal bars of color made with highlighters are a good device.

As a class or individually, students may want to make smaller, more specific time lines. Inventions of the Industrial Revolution, social history, or Native American history are topics to consider. In addition, Resource Pages 3 (TG page 95) and 7 (TG page 99) give students an opportunity to plot key foreign policy events on time lines. Encourage students to look for cause-and-effect trends in all of their time lines.

Assessment/Sequencing When students have completed the class and individual time lines, have them use events on the time line to revise their graphic organizers and make judgments about the growing sectionalism over issues such as slavery, Native American lands, states' rights, and political parties.

USING MAPS

Students should trace the changes and conflicts in Book Four on a large classroom map as well as on individual maps: one that

USING THE RESOURCE MAPS

At the back of this guide you will find blank reproducible maps that accompany activities from the Teaching Guide and Student Study Guide. Also, you will find reference maps you may choose to hand out to assist students in completing map research projects.

shows mountain ranges and river systems would be best. Always encourage students to locate the actions they're reading about and to think about the implications of geography upon those events.

For this period of expansion and development, have students create a series of maps, one for each decade, that show the changes taking place. They should show states as they form, new territories as they're added, and changes in the political status of neighbors. These maps can become part of the large classroom time line or be made into individual time lines.

Assessment/Analyzing Maps   Set up a large outline map of the United States. Have students label the main regions. (*North, South, West*) Then ask them to illustrate the map with people or symbols that reveal the essential character of each region and key historical events that took place there.

WRITING HISTORY

Help students make American history their own by encouraging them to retell and add to the stories in *A History of US*. One way to accomplish this is to ask students to write their own history books in their History Journals.

When you finish each chapter, give students time to write their own accounts of the events. (Some students may want to illustrate their histories, too.) Encourage them to do additional research online or at the library media center, to look into topics that interest them. (Point out that Joy Hakim often suggests ideas for further investigation.) From time to time, ask volunteers to share their histories with the class.

Assessment/Editing Historical Writing   When students have finished compiling their own history books for each Part, have them exchange these books with other students. Challenge students to pick one or two chapters in their classmate's book for editing. On a separate sheet of paper, students can list suggestions for needed clarifications or other improvements. They should also note well-written or especially interesting selections. Student editors should meet with "authors" to discuss the changes. After "authors" have revised their work, call on volunteers to read their revised history chapters aloud. Encourage them to note the tips that helped improve their writing.

TEACHING HISTORY

Assign teams of students to work cooperatively to teach portions of the book. Remind students that the best teaching and learning occurs when everyone is involved. Students should think beyond the lecture format. Encourage them to enrich their instruction with pictures, poems, art, and so on. The "teachers" should also devise short homework assignments or in-class activities. At the end of the lesson, they should submit several questions to be used as part of a self-evaluation test.

Assessment/Self-Analysis   If students have acted as teachers for their class, ask them to evaluate their own teaching techniques. What worked best? What would they do differently for the next book in *A History of US*?

THE BIG IDEAS

In 1790 Noah Webster, author of the first American English Dictionary, believed it was time for Americans to correct the mistakes of our English past–from our spelling to our national character. He wrote:

> *Americans, unshackle your minds and act like independent beings….You have an empire to raise and support by your exertions and a national character to establish and extend by your wisdom and virtues….Americans must believe and act from the belief that it is dishonorable to waste life in mimicking the follies of other nations….*

For Americans it was a time of change. They were the people and theirs was the time to right the wrongs of the past. Eager to put their ideas into practice, they set to work. The first results are the subject of Part 1.

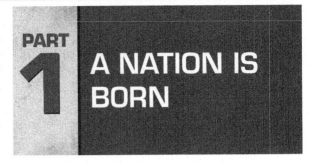

PART 1 — A NATION IS BORN

INTRODUCING PART 1

SETTING GOALS

Introduce Part 1 by writing its title, "A Nation Is Born," on the chalkboard. Discuss the idea of birth and what that means for a nation. *(Students should understand that what is "born" is a new government—usually one that is unlike what preceded it in many ways.)* Ask students why a new nation might be a difficult place and time in which to live. *(Everything a new nation does, it does for the first time. The people of a new nation must often find their way through trial and error.)* Then ask students why living in the newly formed United States would be exciting. *(Students may say that living in the new nation would be exciting because people had a chance to participate in a totally new, untried form of government.)*

To set goals for Part 1, tell students that they will
*   describe the roles of George Washington, John Adams, Thomas Jefferson, Alexander Hamilton, and Benjamin Banneker in the formation of the new nation.
*   debate liberal and conservative views of government.
*   describe the early history of the nation's capital city.
*   analyze information from the first United States census.

SETTING A CONTEXT FOR READING

Thinking About the Big Ideas   To illustrate the task of the first administration, ask students to imagine the building of a structure that is different from anything ever built before. The builders have a blueprint, but now they have to follow the plan. What if two builders disagree? One says that the strength is in the crossbeams; the other says it is the uprights that will make the structure strong. The neighbors think that they are both crazy and that the building will surely fall. But both builders are sure of one thing: If their building stands, it will change how all buildings are made.

Explain that this was the situation in the United States in 1790. The Constitution was the plan; the new structure was a modern democratic government. As the new nation forged its identity, who would hold power—and what kind of power? Ask students to imagine how Americans and Europeans felt. Who might be worried, and who might be interested in the outcome? How might what was happening in the United States affect governments in the rest of the world?

Interpreting Pictures   Have students look closely at the painting of George Washington's home on pages 14-15. Ask them to examine the details of the American President's life, such as how people are dressed, and to observe the artist's style of painting. Then have them turn to page 18 and examine the painting of King Charles IV of Spain. Ask: How do the paintings differ? *(The American painting is simpler compared to the rich, realistic detail of the Spanish painting. The Americans are dressed simply in plain fabrics while the members of the royal family are richly dressed in fancy fabrics and jewelry.)* Then have students preview all of the pictures in Part 1. Based on the pictures, have students make predictions about how this new nation will be different from the nations of Europe. *(Students may predict that the people and leaders of the new nation will be less wealthy but more free thinking than the people and leaders of European nations.)*

SETTING A CONTEXT IN SPACE AND TIME
Using Maps   Ask students to point out on a wall map of the United States today the area that constituted the nation 200 years ago. Have students turn to the U.S. census of 1790 map on page 34 and describe the nation as it was then. Where did the European and African-Americans live? *(along the East Coast)* Which states were the most populated? *(those first settled, such as Virginia)* Have students look at the art and conjecture who lived in the Northwest and Southwest territories. *(The art shows an Ojibwa dwelling in the Northwest and a Cherokee cabin in the Southwest.)*

The small city maps along the bottom of the page show three major cities. Ask the students what element is common to all three. *(They are all ports with access to the Atlantic Ocean.)* Discuss why this would be an important attribute for a growing city.

Understanding Change over Time   Remind students that the Constitution created an entirely new system of government. Ask them to think about all of the "firsts" that would be required for the new nation to work. Ask students to turn to the Chronology on page 181. Have them identify any "firsts" they see in the initial four listings. *(first president; first census)* Suggest that students design a symbol to stand for "firsts" and use it on their class time line as they read about these and other groundbreaking events in Part 1.

USING THE RUBRICS

To assess these writing assignments, group projects, and activities, scoring rubrics have been provided at the back to this Teaching Guide. Be sure to explain the rubrics to your students.

THE FATHER OF OUR COUNTRY

PAGES 13-19

1 Class Period   Homework: Student Study Guide p. 11

Chapter Summary

The nation's first presidential election resulted in the only unanimous vote in our history. Having led the revolution, George Washington was the popular choice to lead the nation.

Key Vocabulary

tsars   monarchy   armory
inauguration   president elect

1. CONNECT

Help students make judgments about George Washington as a political leader and founding father by asking them to identify and describe their favorite presidents or political leaders. Discuss the character traits of great leaders.

2. UNDERSTAND

1. Read pages 13-17. Discuss: What means of transportation did George Washington use to travel from Mount Vernon to New York? *(carriage, horseback, barge)*
2. Read the rest of the chapter. Discuss: Why were kings, queens, and tsars around the globe "shivering in their shoes"? *(The American Revolution showed these rulers that they could lose their thrones; the French Revolution showed them that they could also lose their heads!)*
3. Why was George Washington so popular? *(because of his heroic role during the Revolutionary War, and his likable character, wisdom, modesty, and politeness.)*

3. CHECK UNDERSTANDING

Writing   Have students imagine that they are reporters in 1789. Ask them to write a one-paragraph news article about George Washington from the time he leaves his home in Mount Vernon to his inauguration.

Thinking About the Chapter (Analyzing)   Have the class discuss what Washington meant when he wrote in his diary: "About ten o'clock I bade farewell to Mount Vernon, to private life, and to domestic felicity, and with a mind oppressed with more anxious and painful sensations than I have words to express, set out for New York." *(Students should realize that Washington, who loved his home, was leaving for what he probably feared would be a painfully difficult and challenging job.)*

NOTE TO THE TEACHER
When you see the instruction "Read...," you can interpret it in any way that fits the lesson you are creating for your students. For example, you may read aloud to the class or to small groups, you may have volunteers read aloud, or you may have the class read silently.

READING NONFICTION

Analyzing Word Choice

Have students find words the author uses to describe Washington (*gracious, modest*) and then read Abigail Adams's description on page 14. Ask partners to find and list synonyms the author uses for each word used by Adams; for example, *polite/gracious*. Then discuss how these word choices help readers know that the author and Adams share similar points of view about Washington's character.

MORE ABOUT...

George Washington

In *The Great Experiment; George Washington and the American Republic,* historian John Rhodehamel wrote: "Washington was not a traditional military hero....He was not a military genius....The real source of Washington's greatness lay in his moral character. Washington was a man of virtue, but this virtue was not given to him by nature. He had to work for it, to cultivate it, and his contemporaries knew that he did. Washington was a self-made hero."

HISTORY ARCHIVES

A History of US Sourcebook

#23, George Washington, *Inaugural Address* (1789)

A History of US Sourcebook

1. #24, George Washington, *Letter to Moses Seixas* (1790)

2. #25, George Washington, *Letter to the New Church in Baltimore* (1793)

LINKING DISCIPLINES

History/Science

In 1793 there were two kinds of balloons, hot-air balloons and hydrogen balloons. Blanchard's balloon was filled with hydrogen gas. Challenge students to research and describe why hydrogen balloons fly, and how they descend back to earth.

MORE ABOUT...

Jean-Pierre Francois Blanchard

The well-known Dr. Benjamin Rush wrote this in a letter to a friend: "For some time days past the conversation in our city has turned wholly upon Mr. Blanchard's late Aerial Voyage. It was truly a sublime sight. Every faculty of the mind was seized, expanded and captivated by it, 40,000 people concentrating their eyes and thoughts at the same instant, upon the same object, and all deriving nearly the same degree of pleasure from it."

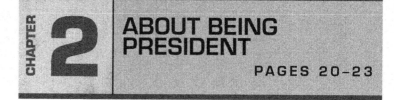

CHAPTER 2 — ABOUT BEING PRESIDENT

PAGES 20-23

1 Class Period   Homework: Student Study Guide p. 12

Chapter Summary

Every decision made by the new president set a precedent. When Washington chose advisers, the nation's first cabinet was born.

Key Vocabulary

precedent	executive	legislative
judicial	cabinet	dictatorship

1. CONNECT

Tell students that it was said of Washington that he was "first in war, first in peace, and first in the hearts of his countrymen." Ask what they already know about Washington that would explain this statement. (*Washington led the American forces in the revolution. He was the first president of the United States. He was so popular that he was the only president elected unanimously.*)

2. UNDERSTAND

1. Read to the end of pages 21-22 up to "When he needed help writing…." Ask: How was the first cabinet formed and what was its purpose? (*Washington appointed secretaries to advise him. Together they were called the cabinet.*)
2. Read the rest of the chapter. Discuss: How did Washington's views on political parties differ from Madison's? (*Washington called parties factions and thought that they caused conflict. Madison felt that factions should be encouraged in a democracy to balance power and prevent one group from controlling the government.*)

3. CHECK UNDERSTANDING

Writing   Ask students to write a one-paragraph description of Washington's presidency. What firsts did he achieve, and what problems did he face?

Thinking About the Chapter (Recognizing Points of View) The author describes Washington's point of view on several topics. Challenge students to identify them. (*Washington thought that the president should be grand, that it was important for Americans to meet their president, that the presidency was serious business, and that political parties caused conflict.*)

1 Class Period   **Homework: Student Study Guide p. 13**

Chapter Summary

Hamilton and Jefferson, two great forces in American political thought, were at odds, so America's party system was born.

Key Vocabulary

Federalist	Democratic-Republican	conservative
liberal	capitalist	capital
credit	collateral	bond
interest	invest	free enterprise system

1. CONNECT

Remind students that the first American political parties formed during Washington's presidency. Ask students to review Washington's views on political parties. *(He thought they caused conflict.)* Discuss how political parties can create both choice and conflict.

2. UNDERSTAND

1. Read pages 24-27. Discuss: How did Jefferson and Hamilton differ regarding the abuse of power?. *(Jefferson feared strong government; Hamilton feared the masses.)*

2. Read the rest of the chapter. Discuss: How did Hamilton give the United States a good credit rating? *(He forced Congress to pay off debts.)*

3. Read the feature on pages 28-29. Use Resource Page 1 (TG page 107) to have students identify and compare the opinions of Federalists and Democratic-Republicans on protective tariffs, banking, and payment of the states' war debts.

4. To aid student understanding of differing points of view among political parties, discuss differences among contemporary political parties. Have the class select several current issues, then identify the points of view of major parties on each issue. Encourage groups to do outside research using newspapers, television, and other media.

3. CHECK UNDERSTANDING

Writing   Ask students to imagine that they are living in 1790, Would they have been conservatives or a liberals? Ask them to write a paragraph explaining their views on key issues in 1790.

Thinking About the Chapter (Making Judgments)   Discuss the author's questions: How do you balance liberty and power? How do you guarantee freedom? *(Students should consider recent events in which civil liberties were at issue.)*

HISTORY ARCHIVES

A History of US Sourcebook
#26, From George Washington, *Farewell Address* (1796)

MEETING INDIVIDUAL NEEDS

Pair visual learners and ESL students with their more verbal counterparts. Then have each pair describe what they see in the cartoon of Thomas Jefferson on page 26. (*The Federal eagle is snatching the U.S. Constitution from Jefferson, who is about to throw the document into a fire.*) Have pairs analyze the cartoon's message. (*The cartoon is criticizing Jefferson's ideas as being contrary to the Constitution.*) Have each pair create its own historical or contemporary political cartoon.

MORE ABOUT...

Money

Before Alexander Hamilton began to straighten things out, money changed value from state to state, or even from one town to the next! When Washington traveled to New York City, a shilling (there was no U.S. currency yet) was worth 15 pennies in Philadelphia, 30 pennies in Trenton, New Jersey, 24 pennies in nearby Princeton, and 21 pennies in New York City!

LINKING DISCIPLINES

History/Economics

The free-enterprise system began emerging in our nation in the early 1800s, as the economy shifted from agriculture to industry and business. Have students discuss the early farming and landholding economy. Challenge them to predict changes that might occur as the United States entered a free-enterprise money economy. What would the characteristics of the free enterprise system be? (*Thousands of Americans would leave farms and villages to earn money working in factories in towns and cities. Factories would produce more and more goods as people earned money to buy the goods. Businessmen would invest money to expand businesses and industry.*)

MORE ABOUT...

The Capital

Before Washington became the nation's capital, the seat of government moved nine times! Philadelphia was the first capital, and then Baltimore. During the Revolution, the government had to move to Lancaster and then York in Pennsylvania. Then it moved to Trenton and Princeton in New Jersey and Annapolis, in Maryland. After the war, New York City became the capital, then Philadelphia again, before it finally settled in Washington in 1800.

GEOGRAPHY CONNECTIONS

The site of the Federal City was very close to the center of the U.S. population. Have students use a wall map of the United States to identify the centers of the population as follows: 1790, 23 miles east of Baltimore; 1800, 18 miles west of Baltimore; 1900, near Columbus, Indiana. Ask students to determine the location of a new Federal City if it were to be based on our population center today.

---

1 Class Period   **Homework: Student Study Guide p. 14**

Chapter Summary

What befits a new nation more than a new capital? A central location on federal ground calmed state jealousies.

Key Vocabulary

capital   Capitol

1. CONNECT

Ask students who have visited Washington, D.C., to describe the city. Then discuss the causes and effects of centralizing a nation's power in one city.

2. UNDERSTAND

1. Read pages 30-31 up to "A Quaker abolitionist...." Discuss: Why was the site on the Potomac River chosen for the new capital? *(The central location resolved jealousies.)*
2. Read the rest of the chapter. Ask: How was the new nation's capital city planned? What roles did Andrew Ellicott, Benjamin Banneker, and Pierre L'Enfant play in that planning? *(Land was surveyed by Ellicott and his assistant Banneker. L'Enfant designed the center of the new capital. Contests were held to find the best plans for the President's House and the Capitol building.)*

3. CHECK UNDERSTANDING

Writing Ask students to write a paragraph describing the sequence of events and key figures in the creation of the nation's new capital.

Thinking About the Chapter (Interpreting a Historical Map) Turn students' attention to the map and city plan of Washington on page 31. Discuss the plan. Have students locate the Capitol and the President's House, the only two buildings drawn on the plan. Discuss why, instead of a simple grid or a city based on squares, the designers planned avenues that radiated out from these two buildings and other circles, like spokes of wheels. *(With this plan, the two imposing structures could be admired at the end of many wide avenues.)*

5 COUNTING NOSES

PAGES 33–36

1 Class Period Homework: Student Study Guide p. 15

Chapter Summary
Since representative government is based on numbers of people, the government's first task was to count its population.

Key Vocabulary
census inhabitants

1. CONNECT

Ask students what they know about the U.S. Census. Have they been counted yet? Explain that 2000 and 2010 are census years. Discuss how and why the census is taken every 10 years.

2. UNDERSTAND

1. Read page 33. Discuss: Who was and was not counted in the 1790 census? (*European and African men, women, and children—both free and enslaved—were counted. Native Americans were not.*)
2. Read the rest of the chapter. Discuss: If fewer people lived in cities, why were cities important? (*As they are now, cities were centers of trade and communication. As ports, they were more international and the entry points into the new nation.*)

3. CHECK UNDERSTANDING

Writing Ask students to imagine that they are reporters in 1790. Their assignment is to write a short article on the just-published first census of the United States.

Thinking About the Chapter (Categorizing Information)
Have students organize the census data about 1790 and 1800 in two lists on the chalkboard, or have students create their own lists during the discussion. (*1790—4 million people, 697,681 enslaved, 95 percent on farms; 1800—5.3 million people, 1 million blacks, 1 million people on frontier*)

READING NONFICTION
Analyzing Text Features
Have students identify the chapter number and title on page 33. Help them understand that in this chapter (and the book as a whole), the author discusses one main idea in a few pages, and does not use subheads. Ask students to identify the main idea here (*how and why the first and subsequent U.S. censuses were held*) and tell how the illustrations, captions, map, and sidebars give more information about this subject.

ACTIVITIES/JOHNS HOPKINS TEAM LEARNING
See the Student Team Learning Activity on TG page 34.

GEOGRAPHY CONNECTIONS
Have students turn to the map on page 34 and describe the locations of U.S. cities in 1790. (*along the East Coast*) Ask: Where was the frontier? (*east of the Mississippi River in the Northwest Territory, Kentucky, the Southwest Territory, and western Georgia*)

JOHNS HOPKINS TEAM LEARNING

STAND UP AND BE COUNTED

1 EXTENDED CLASS PERIOD

JOHNS HOPKINS
U N I V E R S I T Y

FOCUS ACTIVITY

1. Elicit what students know about how members of the House of Representatives are selected today, including how many representatives your state has and any effects the 2000 Census may have had on that number.

2. Have students form partnerships to **Partner Read** Article 1, Sections 1 and 2 of the Constitution on pages 59-60 of *A History of US Sourcebook*.

3. Ask each partnership to locate the answers to these questions: How often do people select representatives? *(every two years)* On what basis was the number of representatives determined? *(the state's free population, excluding Native Americans and counting enslaved people as three-fifths of a person)* What was the minimum number of representatives a state could have? *(one)*

STUDENT TEAM LEARNING ACTIVITY/INTERPRETING CENSUS DATA

1. Create teams of four students each. Tell teams that they will be reading and interpreting information about U.S. Census data and the House of Representatives.

2. Distribute Resource Page 2 (TG page 108) to each team. Tell team members to read the page together.

3. Write the following questions on the chalkboard, and ask each team to use Resource Page 2 to answer them.
- How many members attended the First Congress? *(59)*
- Why did North Carolina and Rhode Island have no representatives? *(Neither state had ratified the Constitution yet.)*
- Which states have gained representatives in 200 years? *(Georgia, Maryland, Massachusetts, New Jersey, New York, North Carolina, Pennsylvania, Rhode Island)*
- Which states had the same number of representatives in the 107th Congress as they had in the First Congress? *(Connecticut, Delaware, South Carolina)*
- Which states lost representatives? *(New Hampshire, Virginia)*
- How could states lose representatives or have the same number if they gained in population? *(Today, each House member represents more citizens than in 1790.)*

4. Circulate and Monitor As teams work, systematically visit them. Be sure that they understand that Article 1, Section 2 of the Constitution assigns the number of representatives for each state for three years and calls for a census. If necessary, help them interpret Resource Page 2 by asking and answering questions. Check that students are completing the assignment in a timely, accurate, and complete manner.

5. Sharing Information As much as possible have each team share their answer to one of the questions with the class, while all teams check and revise their answers as needed.

ASSESSMENT

Part 1 Check-Up   Use Check-Up 1 (TG page 100) to assess student learning in Part 1.

ALTERNATE ASSESSMENT
Ask students to write an essay answering the following question, which links the big ideas across chapters:

Making Connections   Think about the passions, hopes, and fears of Americans as they created not only a new government, but a new way of governing. Imagine that you were an American in 1790. How would you feel about your country? Suppose you met someone from England who said that your government would not last a year. What would you reply? *(Students should realize that Americans were overwhelmingly optimistic about the outcome of their experiment in democracy. Many felt as Thomas Paine described in* Common Sense: *"the birthday of a new world is at hand.")*

DEBATING THE ISSUES
Use the topic below to stimulate debate.

Resolved   That power leads to oppression. *(Ask students to debate as Hamilton and Jefferson might have. You may wish to extend the debate to include opinions on other topics, such as the national debt and public education.)*

MAKING ETHICAL JUDGMENTS
The following activity asks students to consider issues of ethics.

Read aloud the quote from a letter Washington wrote to his close friend Henry Knox days before he left his home for public office:

> *"…my movements to the chair of government will be accompanied by feelings not unlike those of a culprit, who is going to the place of his execution; so unwilling am I, in the evening of a life nearly consumed in public cares, to quit a peaceful abode for an ocean of difficulties.…"*

Have students describe in their own words the meaning of the passage, discussing the difficult choice between personal needs and civic duty. Then ask them to think of careers today that they might choose to help their community.

PROJECTS AND ACTIVITIES
Drawing a Route Map   Students can work in groups to draw a linear map of Washington's journey from Mount Vernon to New York, showing the landmarks on his way. Suggest that they draw the route as a straight line on a long piece of butcher paper. They can draw Mount Vernon on the far left, and the Federal Court House in New York City at the far right. The road with elements from the story lies in between.

USING THE RUBRICS

To assess these writing assignments, group projects, and activities, scoring rubrics have been provided at the back to this Teaching Guide. Be sure to explain the rubrics to your students.

NOTE FROM THE AUTHOR

Learning to do research is an important lifetime skill. Send your students to the library to find out more about the people in this period in history. Have them choose a character, write about her or him, and be prepared to read their stories out loud.

LOOKING AHEAD

Paraphrasing and Predicting

Tell students that before he left office, George Washington gave the nation the following advice and warning:

> *In offering to you, my countrymen, these counsels of an old and affectionate friend,... [I hope] that they may now and then recur to moderate the fury of party spirit, to warn against the mischiefs of foreign intrigue, [and] to guard against the impostures of pretended patriotism.*

Ask students to rephrase Washington's advice in their own words. Will Americans follow all of this advice? Some of it? Or none at all? Tell students that in Part 2 they will learn the answer.

Designing a Capitol Building   Remind students how plans for the Capitol were chosen. Then hold another contest in which students design a new Capitol building for the modern world. Suggest that they include solar heating, wind generators, atriums, or other innovations in their plans.

Designing Money and Stamps   Point out that the new government needed to make stamps and money. Ask students to design something appropriate for 1790.

Linking Past and Present   Remind students that the site for the District of Columbia was chosen because it was centrally located. Have them find the geographic center of the continental United States on a modern map. About how far is that center from the District of Columbia?

Writing a Letter   Point out that many young Americans in the 1790s had relatives in England. Ask students to write a letter to an English cousin describing their new government. Remind the students that many Europeans thought that the new government would quickly fail.

Writing a Poem for the Inauguration   Explain that it is a tradition for a noted poet to read a poem at the inauguration of the president. Have students write a poem for the inauguration of George Washington. It can be about the president or the occasion.

Looking Deeper into History   Have students reread the story of Jean-Pierre François Blanchard and his balloon flight (Book 4, page 23), then research information about ballooning and other early experiments in flight in America. Have students present their findings in a report or in drawings.

Graphing the National Debt   The national debt is an issue in current events. Have students research the amount of the present debt and make a bar graph or pictograph to compare it with the following information for 1790: foreign debt, $12 million, domestic debt (including state debts), $69 million.

THE BIG IDEAS

After his inauguration in 1797, President John Adams wrote to his wife Abigail. While confiding in her his dread of public speaking, he wrote of a greater fear:

> *Jealousies and rivalries have…never stared me in the face in such horrid forms as at present. I see how the thing is going. At the next election England will set up…Hamilton, and France, Jefferson.…*

Foreign struggles continued to pull at Americans, and factions grew more passionate. Then, when the eighteenth century gave way to the nineteenth, the Federalist Era was ended by Jefferson and the Democratic-Republicans. Jefferson believed power would shift to the common man and called it a second revolution. Part 2 describes these forces that molded the nation.

INTRODUCING PART 2

SETTING GOALS
Introduce Part 2 by writing its title, "Shaping the New Nation," on the chalkboard. Ask students what might need to be "shaped" in a new nation. (*Possible responses: monetary system, postal services, foreign policy, national security, taxes*)

To set goals for Part 2, tell students that they will
- describe the roles and importance of John Adams, John Marshall, and Thomas Jefferson.
- debate conservative and liberal views of government.
- identify the roles played by key figures in the Lewis and Clark expedition.

SETTING A CONTEXT FOR READING
Thinking About the Big Ideas   Throughout history the violence of revolutions has often led to further violence. When one power is overthrown, there is a struggle to fill its place. Americans were lucky to have founded a system that worked well. As power changed hands in the new nation, there was no violence, but there was conflict. Ask students to recall the ideological conflicts between Hamilton and Jefferson described in Part 1. Tell them that the next two presidents will be a Federalist and a Democratic-Republican. Ask students to recall political disputes in recent elections in similar terms.

Categorizing Information   As students read chapters 6-11, they will come across the viewpoints of Federalists and Democratic-Republicans. Have students make a three-column chart in their notebooks with the headings *Issue, Federalist View,* and *Democratic-Republican View.* As students encounter a viewpoint on an issue such as the function of government, courts, banks, foreign affairs, or the American people, have them use the information to fill in the chart.

PART 2 SHAPING THE NEW NATION

SETTING A CONTEXT IN SPACE AND TIME

Using Maps   To illustrate the great geographical change that would take place in 1803, have students first review the map showing the United States in 1790 on page 34. Ask students to describe what was west of the Mississippi River, who lived there, and which country claimed control of it. Then have them turn to the map on pages 60-61. Ask students to describe Louisiana—its people, its geography, and its animals—using the information on the map. Have students predict how the acquisition of this vast region might change the young republic.

Understanding Change over Time   The calendar was about to turn a century—almost always a time of change. Point out besides showing specific events, time lines can also show periods of time or eras. For example, the Federalist Era began in 1789 with the inauguration of George Washington. As 1800 came to a close, that era was ending. Have students mark the Federalist Era on their time lines by using a bar running from 1789 through 1800 and labeling it on the time line or in a legend. As students read Part 2, have them identify the political era that began in 1801 (*Democratic-Republican, or the Age of Jefferson*) and mark it in a similar fashion on their time lines.

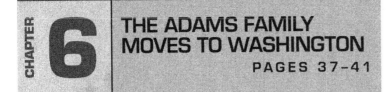

CHAPTER **6** THE ADAMS FAMILY MOVES TO WASHINGTON
PAGES 37–41

1 Class Period   Homework: Student Study Guide p. 16

Chapter Summary
As John Adams and his administration adjusted to life in the Federal City, news of George Washington 's death plunged the nation into mourning.

Key Vocabulary
Executive Mansion   Oval Office

1. CONNECT

Ask students to describe what they already know about John Adams and his wife, Abigail Adams. Direct their attention to page 37, where the author reminds us that John Adams was "that solid thinker from Massachusetts who helped convince Thomas Jefferson to write the Declaration of Independence," and that Abigail Adams was "a strong woman who liked to write letters."

2. UNDERSTAND

1. Read pages 37-39. Discuss: If the city of Washington was surrounded by woods, why was firewood a big problem for John and Abigail Adams? *(The President's house was big and damp, so lots of firewood was needed. John Adams would not have slaves and there were few laborers in the new city, so firewood was very expensive.)*
2. Read the special feature on pages 40-41. Discuss: What are some of the strangest uses of rooms in the White House? *(Responses will vary. One example is John Quincy Adams keeping a pet alligator in the East Room.)*

3. CHECK UNDERSTANDING

Writing   Ask students to write a one-paragraph description of life in the White House in 1797.

Thinking About the Chapter (Synthesizing)   Have the class discuss why the Americans decided in 1799 to give the name Washington to the unfinished Federal City. *(George Washington was viewed by many almost as a god or saint, and they wanted to honor him; they were also shocked and saddened by his death and wanted to commemorate their hero.)*

LINKING DISCIPLINES

History/Health

Ask interested students to find out more about how people were bled. They will discover that one of two methods was used. A vein was punctured using a small sharp blade or scarificator, which was a sharp tool that prevented the doctor from making too deep a cut. Probably safer (though perhaps creepier to some) was the use of the common leech to suck blood. Leeches were widely available in the mud of streams and lakes.

MORE ABOUT...

Washington

In his will, Washington wrote: "It is my Will and desire that all the Slaves which I hold in my own right, shall receive their freedom." He went on to say that the elderly freed slaves should be cared for by his heirs, that young children without families should be taught a skill, and, most unusual for that time, that the children be taught to read and write.

CHAPTER 7

READING NONFICTION

Analyzing Point of View

The author says that in her opinion, John Adams was a great man, but just passable as president. Ask students to find the evidence the author gives to support her point of view.

(Hakim quotes primary sources, such as Benjamin Franklin, Thomas Jefferson, and John Adams, as well as a secondary source—a quote from historian Joseph Ellis.)

ABOUT PRESIDENT ADAMS

PAGES 42-44

1 Class Period   **Homework: Student Study Guide p. 17**

Chapter Summary

John Adams succeeded in keeping the republic out of war in Europe, but he failed to stop the trend toward factionalism at home.

Key Vocabulary

diplomat   republicanism   protocol

1. CONNECT

Discuss the problems the first president of the United States faced, including factionalism. Then ask students to predict how Adams's presidency will be different than Washington's.

2. UNDERSTAND

1. Read the chapter. Discuss: Contrast how Jefferson and Adams viewed democracy and the masses. *(Jefferson believed in democracy or government by the people. Although Adams believed in representative government, he didn't trust the masses or democracy; he thought that the wealthy, educated segments of society should govern.)*
2. Ask: In his farewell address, Washington warned Americans to stay out of foreign affairs and to avoid fighting between parties. How do you think Washington would have felt about Adams's administration? *(Washington would probably have approved of Adams for keeping the nation out of war, but he would have faulted him for his inability to stop fighting between parties.)*

3. CHECK UNDERSTANDING

Writing   Have students write one paragraph that summarizes the author's opinion of John Adams as a person and president.

Thinking About the Chapter (Distinguishing Between Fact and Opinion)   Have students review the chapter and categorize each piece of information as fact or opinion. *(Students should find that the chapter presents mostly opinions and only a few facts.)*

<table>
<tr><td>CHAPTER
8</td><td>**ALIEN AND SEDITION:
AWFUL AND SORRY**
PAGES 45–47</td></tr>
</table>

<table>
<tr><td>CHAPTER
9</td><td>**SOMETHING IMPORTANT:
JUDICIAL REVIEW**
PAGES 48–51</td></tr>
</table>

1 Class Period   Homework: Student Study Guide pp. 18–19

Chapter Summaries

Afraid that French influence and Democratic-Republicans were a threat to the republic, the Federalists passed laws limiting freedoms. The unpopular laws pointed up the need for a stronger judicial system to check laws passed by Congress. John Marshall initiated judicial review.

Key Vocabulary

Alien and Sedition acts   excises
checks and balances   judicial review

1. CONNECT

Be sure that students understand that *alien* here means "foreigner." Have a volunteer look up the word and read the definition to the class. Then ask students to describe what they know about aliens living in the United States today.

2. UNDERSTAND

1. Read Chapter 8. Ask: What were the Alien and Sedition acts? Why did so many Americans oppose these acts? *(The Alien acts made it hard for aliens to become U.S. citizens and easy for them to be thrown out of the country. The Sedition Act made it a crime to criticize the government. Many Americans believed strongly (and correctly) that the acts were unconstitutional.)*
2. Read Chapter 9. Ask: How did John Marshall help protect those freedoms guaranteed in the Bill of Rights from laws like the Sedition Act? *(He initiated a process called judicial review, which gave the Supreme Court the power to declare laws unconstitutional.)*
3. Have students study two of John Marshall's landmark judicial opinions—in *Marbury* v *Madison* (*Sourcebook pp. 102-103*) and *McCulloch* v *Maryland* (*Sourcebook pp 108-110*). Students should work in study groups to analyze and summarize the issues behind each decision and the decisions themselves.(*In* Marbury *v* Madison, *students should note that the central issue involved the validity of an act of Con-*

HISTORY ARCHIVES

A History of US Sourcebook

1. #29, From John Marshall, opinion in *Marbury v. Madison* (1803)

2. #32, From John Marshall, opinion in *McCulloch v. Maryland* (1819)

ACTIVITIES/JOHNS HOPKINS TEAM LEARNING

See the Student Team Learning Activity on TG page 45.

MORE ABOUT...

Names of Court Cases

The first name in the title of a court case identifies the plaintiff, or person or party that is bringing a complaint or accusation before the court. The v. stands for versus, which means "against." The last name is the defendant, or the party that is accused. In *Marbury* v. *Madison*, the plaintiff William Marbury felt he had been wronged by Secretary of State James Madison. So Marbury (plaintiff) brought a suit against Madison (defendant).

MEETING INDIVIDUAL NEEDS

You can use this chapter to have students write poems about what it feels like to be discriminated against.

gress—the Judiciary Act—to force action by the President. The Supreme Court declared the Judiciary Act unconstitutional and affirmed that the Constitution is the highest law of the land. In McCulloch *v* Maryland, *the issues again involved Congressional power. The state of Maryland questioned the right of Congress to establish a national bank. The Court ruled that it did have that right. In the same opinion, the Court ruled that a state could not impose a tax on a federal agency; in this case, Maryland could not tax the Second Bank of the United States. The case established the principle of national supremacy.)*

3. CHECK UNDERSTANDING

Writing   Have students write a short imaginary dialogue on judicial review between John Marshall and Thomas Jefferson.

Thinking About the Chapter (Comparing and Contrasting)
Have the class compare and contrast Marshall's and Jefferson's views on strong federal government, judicial review, and the Alien and Sedition acts. Record students' responses on a Venn diagram. *(Differences: Marshall supported a strong federal government; Jefferson supported state's rights, Marshall supported judicial review, which Jefferson thought made the Court too powerful. Similarities: Both opposed the Alien and Sedition acts.)*

10 MEET MR. JEFFERSON

PAGES 52-56

1 Class Period   **Homework: Student Study Guide p. 20**

Chapter Summary

With the election of Thomas Jefferson, the Federalist Era ended and a quarter-century of Democratic-Republicanism began.

Key Vocabulary

radical   protective tariff

1. CONNECT

Review what students have already learned about Jefferson's accomplishments and character. (*He wrote the Declaration of Independence and was Minister to France, was Washington's Secretary of State and a leader of the Democratic-Republican Party, and was an inventor and supporter of education.*)

2. UNDERSTAND

1. Read pages 52-54 up to "Jefferson believed he was involved in a revolution." Discuss: A person who is *egalitarian* treats people as equals. In what ways was Jefferson egalitarian? (*He preferred informal dinners, sometimes opened the President's House to all citizens, and instructed his staff to treat people as equals whether they were farmers or diplomats.*)
2. Read the rest of the chapter. Discuss: Why did Federalists call Jefferson a radical? (*They were afraid that he was going to continue to make changes until the masses ruled.*)
3. Time Line: Have students complete Resource Page 3 (TG page 109). Then have them compare and contrast the foreign policies of Washington, Adams, and Jefferson.

3. CHECK UNDERSTANDING

Writing   Have students write a one-paragraph report outlining the events of Jefferson's presidency.

Thinking About the Chapter (Summarizing)   Have the class summarize the arguments regarding taxation, protective tariffs, and the banking system. Point out that the two positions are highlighted in the different views held by Jefferson and Hamilton. (Remind students to read the note on the Whiskey Rebellion on page 23.) (*The positions of Jefferson and Hamilton reflected two different financial visions of the nation. Hamilton, who favored an industrialized society and a strong central government, supported high protective tariffs (to protect manufacturers), the whiskey tax, and a national bank. Jefferson hoped for an agricultural society and feared a strong central government. He opposed high protective tariffs as well as the whiskey tax, and was for regional and state banks.*)

READING NONFICTION

Analyzing Primary and Secondary Sources

Remind students that primary sources are records that were created at the time an event took place; they may include written or visual materials, clothing, and objects. Have partners identify and list the primary sources in Chapter 10. (*paintings and drawings, a cartoon, a big cheese poem, an account of making the cheese, direct quotations*) Ask: Why did the author include the cheese-making account instead of telling the story in her own words? (*Possible response: The eyewitness account is livelier and funnier than a retelling.*)

MORE ABOUT...

Jefferson's Dinners

People who were invited to dine with Thomas Jefferson were often surprised at what they were served. Most Americans ate English-style food, but Jefferson liked French and Italian foods. Many of his guests tasted macaroni, olive oil, and Parmesan cheese for the first time. And he was the first President to serve his guests french fries.

READING NONFICTION

Analyzing Text Organization

Have students tell what comparisons the author makes on page 59 about Lewis and Clark. Point out that in this instance, the author discusses Lewis first and then Clark, rather than comparing them point by point.

GEOGRAPHY CONNECTIONS

Have students study Lewis and Clark's journey on the map on pages 60-61 and redraw their route on a wall or reproducible map. (A reproducible map for this activity is at the back of this guide and in the Student Study Guide.) Prompt students to label the map with questions such as these: Where did the journey begin? What Native Americans did they meet or pass along the way? Which rivers did they follow, and what mountains did they cross? What animals did they encounter?

HISTORY ARCHIVES

A History of US Sourcebook

#31, From Meriwether Lewis, *Report to Thomas Jefferson* (1806)

1 Class Period   Homework: Student Study Guide p. 21

Chapter Summary

Jefferson sent Lewis and Clark to explore and study the Louisiana territory in what was possibly the best-organized exploration up to that time.

Key Vocabulary

Northwest Passage

1. CONNECT

Ask students to name their favorite fictional and real-life adventure stories. Discuss elements that make adventure stories enjoyable. Then tell students that they are about to read one of the greatest adventure stories in American history.

2. UNDERSTAND

1. Read pages 57-62 up to "Lewis and Clark went up the Missouri River...." Discuss: Jefferson gave detailed instructions to Lewis and Clark. What information were the explorers expected to gather? (*facts about latitude, longitude, landforms, climate, plant and animal life, soil, minerals, volcanoes, native peoples, and waterways to the Pacific*)
2. Read the rest of the chapter. Discuss: What surprises did the party encounter? (*high mountains, deserts, grizzly bears, endless buffalo herds, unknown plants, and—for Sacajawea—a long-lost brother*)

3. CHECK UNDERSTANDING

Writing   Ask students to imagine they are reporters in St. Louis when Lewis and Clark returned. Have them write a short front-page story about the two-year expedition.

Thinking About the Chapter (Synthesizing)   Have students identify the roles of Lewis, Clark, and Sacajawea during the expedition. (*Lewis, a skilled naturalist, led the party, made careful scientific observations, and kept a journal; Clark was a "people person" and a skilled outdoorsman who drew maps and pictures and wrote a journal; Sacajawea helped the party cross the Rockies by convincing her brother to give the men horses.*)

JOHNS HOPKINS TEAM LEARNING

YOU BE THE JUSTICES

2 CLASS PERIODS

FOCUS ACTIVITY

1. Explain that many recent Supreme Court decisions have focused on the rights of individuals. Ask students to **Brainstorm** what sorts of issues these decisions have involved. *(Students should mention the rights of minorities, women, suspects accused of crimes, aliens, as well as an individual's right to privacy.)*

2. Discuss why the Constitution might be interpreted differently by the Supreme Court today than it was in the early 1800s. Help students to see that as prevailing ideas and opinions about issues change, Supreme Court decisions would reflect those changes.

STUDENT TEAM LEARNING ACTIVITY/PRACTICING JUDICIAL REVIEW

1. Divide the class into teams of four students each. Have teams use **Roundtable** to explain how judicial review has strengthened the Constitution. *(Judicial review enables the Supreme Court to check that laws don't violate the Constitution.)*

2. Distribute a copy of Resource Page 4 (TG page 110) to each team. Tell teams that the page contains accounts of two actual cases that came before the Supreme Court, followed by relevant sections of the Constitution that the Court considered in each case. Explain that after they read each case, team members will review what the Constitution says about the subject. Then team members will discuss each case and make a judgment.

3. Circulate and Monitor As teams work, systematically visit them. If necessary, help students interpret the language of the Constitution. Answer and ask questions, help students resolve difficulties (teams may wish to take a vote), and check that students are completing the assignment in a timely, accurate, and complete manner.

4. When teams have handed down their decisions, you can ask them to research the actual Court decisions in each case. Alternatively, you may wish to explain the Court's rulings to the class.

> ***Brown* v. *Board of Education, Topeka, Kansas, 1954*:** The Supreme Court affirmed the position of the Brown family and claimed that "in the eyes of the law, justice was color-blind." In ruling in favor of Brown, the Court ordered the integration of the country "with all deliberate speed." The civil rights movement had begun!

> ***Tinker* v. *Des Moines, 1969.*** The Supreme Court ruled in favor of the Tinkers, saying, "Students do not shed their constitutional rights at the school house gates." In this case, the court protected what has become known as "symbolic speech."

5. Sharing Information Use **Numbered Heads** to have each team read and explain its decisions to the class.

SUMMARIZING PART 2

Part 2 Check-Up   Use Check-Up 2 (TG page 101) to assess student learning in Part 2.

ALTERNATE ASSESSMENT

Ask students to write an essay answering one of the following questions, which link the big ideas across chapters:

1. Making Connections   The turn of the century marked the beginning of a new identity for Americans. The phrase "We the People" took on a larger meaning. What did it mean in the 1700s? In the 1800s? *(To many in the 1700s, it meant the educated aristocracy. By the 1800s, the phrase came to include the common people.)*

2. Making Connections   How did the power of the presidency change between Washington's term in office and Jefferson's? *(The increased power of the Supreme Court to affect a president's actions through judicial review placed control on the presidency.)*

USING THE RUBRICS

To assess these writing assignments, group projects, and activities, scoring rubrics have been provided at the back to this Teaching Guide. Be sure to explain the rubrics to your students.

DEBATING THE ISSUES

Use the topics below to stimulate debate.

1. Resolved   That people are never good but through necessity. *(Have some students argue the view of John Adams and Alexander Hamilton view. Others should argue Thomas Jefferson's view. Encourage students to see that this debate continues to this day.)*

2. Resolved   That libelous editors should be fined or jailed or both. *(Have students argue for and against freedom of the press. They should include a discussion of the Sedition Act. Bring up issues of libel, racism, and other topics related to freedom of the press.)*

MAKING ETHICAL JUDGMENTS

The following activities ask students to consider issues of ethics.

1. Alexander Hamilton was the leader of the Federalist cause. Yet he chose Republican Jefferson over Federalist Burr for president. Why? *(To focus students' understanding, ask them to think about all of the evidence they have of Hamilton's strong devotion to the good of his country.)*

2. John Adams was a Federalist, but when his party wanted to support England in a war against France, he refused. He was attacked by his own party, as well as by the Democratic-Republicans, because he kept the country neutral. During this difficult time, his wife Abigail was his main support. Write an imaginary dialogue between John and Abigail discussing his decision and his duty as president. *(Dialogues should reflect Adams's dilemma: should he represent his party or the interests of the country as he saw them?)*

PROJECTS AND ACTIVITIES

Writing a Eulogy   Refer students to the poem on page 38. Explain that writings to honor and praise people after their death are called eulogies. Ask students to write a eulogy for Washington.

Writing Historical Fiction   Working individually or in small groups, students can write a fictional account of a family who has moved to the Federalist City. Stories should include descriptions of the geography and living conditions. You might suggest that students look at Abigail Adams's writing for ideas.

Translating Distance into Time   A good way to understand distance is to translate it into time. For example, it is about 1,150 miles from Boston to the Mississippi River, the eastern edge of the Louisiana territory. How long would it have taken a Bostonian to get there in 1803? Give the students the following information and ask them to estimate how long the trip would take: On a flat road a person can walk 4 miles an hour. The distance is 1,150 miles. There are no roads and most of the way is through dense forest. Several mountain ranges and many rivers must be crossed. Time will be needed each day to hunt for and prepare food. *(Students should recognize that such a traveler would be doing well to make the trip in two and a half months.)*

Learning About Art History   When Lewis and Clark returned from their journey, they brought Native American headdresses, clothing, and ornaments. Easterners had never seen this kind of art before. It was a whole new aesthetic to them. Explain that an aesthetic is the way a person or group sees and expresses beauty. Have students research the art of the Plains Indians and then write and illustrate a magazine article based on their findings.

Analyzing Political Slogans   Read aloud—or sing—the following stanzas, from two different sources, to the tune of "Yankee Doodle."

See Johnny at the helm of State,
Head itching for a crowny,
He longs to be, like Georgy, great,
And pull Tom Jeffer downy.

Bold Adams did in Seventy-Six,
Our independence sign, sir,
And he will not give up a jot,
Tho' all the world combine, sir.

Ask students to identify which party sang each song, and to explain its meaning. Students might enjoy adding a stanza to each.

LOOKING AHEAD

Interpreting a Primary Source

Read aloud the following quote from a speech by Tecumseh in 1810.

> [Once] there was no white man on this continent. That it then all belonged to red men, children of the same parents, placed on it by the Great Spirit that made them,...to enjoy its productions, and to fill it with the same race. Once a happy race. Since made miserable by the white people, who are never contented, but always encroaching.

Ask what you can infer from this statement about Indian-white relations on the frontier. (Continued white expansion into Indian territories was causing great stress for the Indians.) What could the Indian people do? Tell students that in Part 3, they will read the stories of three great Indian leaders who devised different strategies for survival.

PART 3
STRATEGIES FOR SURVIVAL

THE BIG IDEAS

In the early 1800s, a Shawnee chief named Tecumseh told a gathering of Native Americans that the only way to stop the white invasion was

…for all the Redmen to unite in claiming a common and equal right in the land, as it was at first and should be yet; for it was never divided, but belongs to all for the use of each.

Conflicts raged as white settlers poured south and west into Indian territories, invading hunting grounds and destroying a way of life. Part 3 tells of the strategies for survival devised by three great chiefs.

INTRODUCING PART 3

SETTING GOALS
Introduce Part 3 by writing its title, "Strategies for Survival," on the chalkboard. Ask students to describe what that phrase means to them. *(survival skills in the wilderness; ways to live a healthful life by eating well and exercising often; strategies for planning for the future by getting a good education and job training)* Then explain that in Part 3, they will find out about different strategies for actual physical survival developed by Native Americans in the early 1800s.

To set goals for Part 3, tell students that they will
- describe three important Native American leaders: Sagoyewatha (Red Jacket), Tekamthi (Tecumseh), and Osceola.
- debate the ethics of European settlers seizing Indian lands.
- map the homelands of the Iroquois, Shawnee, and Seminole.
- evaluate one Indian leader's efforts to unite all Native Americans.

SETTING A CONTEXT FOR READING
Thinking About the Big Ideas   Ask students to consider how they would feel if their "space" were invaded by strangers. What would they do? On the chalkboard, write their responses in a web around the word *invasion*. Then ask students what strategies they would use first. (*Possible responses: Talk to the invaders or call the law.*) What strategies would they use if those failed? (*Possible responses: Find others with the same problem and join forces. Flee, fight, or give in to the invaders.*) How do strategies change when people have more or less power? (*Students may say that people with less power often take more desperate measures.*) Raise the question of identity by asking: How did Native Americans see themselves? (*as the rightful inhabitants of the land*) How did white settlers and government officials see themselves? (*as having a rightful claim to the land*)

Drawing Inferences from Pictures   Ask students to flip through pages 64-75 and examine the portraits. Discuss who the key figures in this Part are. *(Native American chiefs and U.S. military officers)* Then ask students to look at the other paintings. What can they infer from them about the stories in Part 3? *(Key figures, including Native American leaders and the U.S. military, will be involved in a deadly struggle.)* Discuss the information that is revealed by the paintings that would be hard to tell in words. *(The art shows the landscape where the events took place, how people dressed, how they fought, and what weapons they used. It also reveals how close combatants were to one another during battles.)*

SETTING A CONTEXT IN SPACE AND TIME

Using Maps   Have students look at the map on page 71. Tell them that they are going to read about the Iroquois, Shawnee, Creek, and Seminole people. Have students locate each group on the map. Ask students what they notice about the locations of these people. *(They all live on the frontier of the settled American states.)* If students need help arriving at this conclusion, have them indicate on the map the areas where most U.S. citizens lived at the time. Ask students to imagine the state of affairs among the Indians as the new Americans pushed west.

Map Project   As students read the chapters in in this part, you may wish to have them trace locations and routes of native peoples on a wall or reproducible map. Blank reproducible maps and a resource map for this activity can be found at the back of this guide.

Understanding Change over Time   To help students understand the many events occurring simultaneously in the nation, have them research the years 1800-1820. Using their time lines, the chronology on page 181, and other books, students can create for themselves a clear picture of the period.

READING NONFICTION

Analyzing Rhetorical Devices

Discuss that to persuade, a speaker might use loaded words, or words evoking strong emotions, to convince the audience. Have students find loaded words in Red Jacket's speech on pages 64-65). (*Great Spirit, evil day*) Ask: How would these words have affected the Christian ministers whom he was addressing? (*These words would have evoked strong responses; the ideas of "spirit" and "evil" appear in the Bible and are part of Christian teachings.*)

HISTORY ARCHIVES

A History of US Sourcebook

#30, From Red Jacket (Sagoyewatha), *Address to the Chiefs of the Iroquois Confederacy and Missionary Cram*, (1805)

GEOGRAPHY CONNECTIONS

The author wants to know: What is the meaning of Sagoyewatha's phrase "from the rising to the setting sun"? (*He means from the East, where the sun rises, to the West, where it sets.*)

CHAPTER 12

AN ORATOR IN A RED JACKET SPEAKS
PAGES 64-67

1 Class Period   Homework: Student Study Guide p. 22

Chapter Summary

When missionaries threatened the Iroquois way of life, their leader Sagoyewatha (Red Jacket) eloquently asked that his people be granted the same freedom of religion his new neighbors enjoyed.

Key Vocabulary

orator   incorporate

1. CONNECT

Have students describe what they already know about the Iroquois nations (for example, their role in the French and Indian War). Ask: How have Native Americans, up to this point, struggled to keep their lands and cultures?

2. UNDERSTAND

1. Read pages 64-67 up to "Most Americans didn't care...." Discuss: What was Red Jacket asking the missionaries to do? How did he appeal to his audience? (*Red Jacket was asking the missionaries to allow his people to be left alone to worship in their own way. He appealed to the missionaries' memories of their own religious persecution.*)
2. Read the rest of the chapter. Discuss what the author wants to know: Were the missionaries wrong or right to want to share their religion with Native Americans? (*Students may say that the missionaries should have respected Indian beliefs and customs, the way Roger Williams and Sir William Johnson did.*)
3. Map: On Resource Page 5 (TG page 111), have students color in the area in which the Iroquois lived in the early 1800s. (*northern and western New York State*) Ask them to identify the color in the map key.

3. CHECK UNDERSTANDING

Writing   Ask students to write a one-paragraph biography of Red Jacket.

Thinking About the Chapter (Paraphrasing)   Read Red Jacket's speeches on pages 64-67, one paragraph at a time. Have volunteers paraphrase each paragraph. Be sure that students note Red Jacket's use of metaphor on page 67 ("We first knew you a feeble plant..."). Have students select a sentence that they find most eloquent and explain the reason for their choice.

CHAPTER 13 · THE GREAT TEKAMTHI, ALSO CALLED TECUMSEH

PAGES 68–72

1 Class Period   Homework: Student Study Guide p. 23

Chapter Summary

New Americans flooding into the Ohio Valley threatened the lands and lives of the Shawnee people. Tecumseh, a Shawnee leader, clearly saw that all Indian people had to join together as one force or be overwhelmed.

Key Vocabulary

Shakers   shaman

1. CONNECT

Have students recall what they know about Daniel Boone and the Wilderness Road. Remind students that the Wilderness Road led settlers into lands that were home to the Shawnee. Tell students that they are about to meet a great Shawnee leader who tried to protect all Native American lands.

2. UNDERSTAND

1. Read pages 68-70. Discuss: What were Tecumseh's goals, and how did he plan to achieve them? *(Goals: for Indians to return to some traditional ways and keep lands west of the Appalachians. Plan: to unite Indian nations to make a force equal to whites.)*
2. Read the rest of the chapter. Discuss: Tecumseh and Tenskwatawa had different talents, but together they were a force feared by white authorities. What qualities did each bring to their plan? *(Tecumseh: good thinker, speaker, and warrior; Tenskwatawa: powerful shaman or spiritual leader.)*
3. Map: On Resource Page 5 (TG page 111), have students color in Shawnee lands *(a circle covering southern Illinois and Ohio, most of Kentucky, and central Tennessee)* and then update the map key.

3. CHECK UNDERSTANDING

Writing   Ask students to write a one-paragraph biography of Tecumseh.

Thinking About the Chapter (Hypothesizing)   Have the class evaluate what Tecumseh tried to achieve. Was his goal worthy? Why? *(Most students will probably agree with his goal.)* Then have students hypothesize about how American history might have been different if Tecumseh had succeeded.

READING NONFICTION

Analyzing Graphic Aids

Have students use the legend to identify the location of events on the map on page 71. Then ask what the red arrows mean. (*From the title, students should infer that they represent the journeys of Tecumseh.*) Ask students to analyze how the different styles and sizes of type are used to identify locations of states and Native American lands. Ask students to explain how they know that Iowa refers to a people, not the state's name. (*State names are set in a much smaller type; IOWA matches the type style of other Native American peoples on the map.*)

MORE ABOUT...

The Shawnee

Today the Shawnee have land in Oklahoma where they own businesses, farms, and ranches. They live in modern homes, but many still practice traditional ceremonies. Proudly displayed in almost every home is a portrait of Tecumseh.

See the Student Team Learning Activity on
TG page 53.

LINKING DISCIPLINES

Math/Art

Have students calculate the length of the ball-
field described by George Catlin on page 75. Tell
them that a rod is equal to 5.5 yards. Ask them to
draw a scale diagram of the field and label the
distances between each team's goal posts and
the center stake. You may wish to have students
draw the playing areas for modern field sports,
such as soccer, football, and rugby, as a contrast.

MEETING INDIVIDUAL NEEDS

Encourage Spanish-speaking students to contribute to a discussion about American place
names and their relationship to geography and
history. Ask if anyone knows what Pascua Florida
means. (*Spanish name for Easter; literally, "feast
of flowers"*) Explain that Florida is Spanish for
"full of flowers." Have students locate other
Spanish place names on a map of the United
States (*southern and central California, New Mexico, and Texas*). Explain that Spanish settlers
named these places when they settled there.

CHAPTER

14 | OSCEOLA

PAGES 73-75

1 Class Period   Homework: Student Study Guide p. 24

Chapter Summary

For the great Creek nation, the War of 1812 became a civil war.
By the end, both Creek factions suffered grave losses. These
events shaped the childhood of Osceola.

Key Vocabulary
White Sticks   Red Sticks

1. CONNECT

Ask students to describe what they have learned about Florida
history. Have them turn to the map on page 71 to see what
country claimed Florida. (*Spain*) Discuss why Native Americans
who were fighting the United States might flee to Florida.

2. UNDERSTAND

1. Read page 73. Discuss: What caused the Creek nation to
   divide into Red Sticks and White Sticks? (*Some Creeks—the
   White Sticks—wanted to live as whites and cooperate with the
   United States; others—the Red Sticks—wanted to live according to traditional ways and fight against the United States.*)
2. Read the rest of the chapter. Discuss: What qualities did
   young Osceola show that would help him as a man? (*energy,
   determination, honesty, bravery*)
3. Map: On Resource Page 5 (TG page 111), have students
   color in Seminole lands in the early 1800s. (*northern and
   central Florida*) Then have them update the map key.

3. CHECK UNDERSTANDING

Writing   Have students write a one-paragraph description of
Osceola's childhood.

Thinking About the Chapter (Making Predictions)   Ask students what pattern they notice in the relationships between the
United States and Native Americans in these three chapters.
(*Despite their best efforts, the Native Americans were repeatedly
pushed west.*) Ask students to predict what is going to happen to
the Seminole in Florida. (*They too will be forced west.*)

JOHNS HOPKINS TEAM LEARNING

FOUR NATIVE AMERICAN LEADERS MEET

2 CLASS PERIODS

FOCUS ACTIVITY

1. Divide the class into teams of four students each. Ask each team to imagine that they are Creek, Iroquois, Shawnee, or Seminole people in the early 1800s.

2. Have team members brainstorm various strategies that they could use to prevent further loss of land and erosion of their cultures.

STUDENT TEAM LEARNING ACTIVITY/ USING INFORMATION TO CREATE A CONVERSATION SCRIPT

1. Have teams use **Jigsaw** to research and write a conversation script. Assign each team member one of the four Native American leaders: Sagoyewatha, Tecumseh, Tenskwatawa, or Osceola. Students must become experts on their leaders by reviewing the information in Part 3 and locating additional information at the library media center.

2. Give students these questions to guide them in their research:

- What unique character traits did the leader have?
- What was his goal?
- Did he achieve his goals?
- Why or why not?

Experts on a particular leader meet in expert teams before they regroup in their original teams to report their findings.

3. Now ask each team to imagine that the four leaders are meeting to discuss survival strategies. Ask teams to use their expertise to write a conversation script between the four men. Each expert writes his or her leader's part of the script. The leaders must discuss how they feel about settlers taking their land and about their own right to live and believe as they please. They should also debate how best to protect the rights of Native Americans.

4. You may wish to model part of a conversation:
Tecumseh: The only way we can keep our lands is to unite all Indian nations.
Osceola: Yes, but how do we unite when some of our people, such as the White Sticks, defend the United States?

5. Circulate and Monitor As students work, systematically visit each team to help them write a good conversation. Check that each student is contributing to the activity and that the speakers' parts accurately reflect their points of view.

6. Sharing Information After teams have finished their scripts, have them practice their conversations quietly. Then give each team an opportunity to present their conversation to the class.

SUMMARIZING PART 3

Part 3 Check-Up Use Check-Up 3 (TG page 102) to assess student learning in Part 3.

ALTERNATE ASSESSMENT
Ask students to write an essay answering one of the following questions, which link the big ideas across chapters:

1. Making Connections How did each of the following events affect American Indians: (a) Americans win the Revolutionary War; (b) Kentucky, Tennessee, and Ohio become states; (c) the Louisiana Purchase? *(a. Many Native Americans fought for the British because the Americans posed a greater threat to their lands. These Indians were on the losing side at the end of the war. b-c. When territory became part of the United States, both settlers and the U.S. government felt they had the right to take over Indian lands.)*

2. Making Connections Compare the tactics of Red Jacket and Tecumseh in the face of white power. *(Red Jacket counseled waiting, but not accepting white culture. Tecumseh believed that a union of Indian tribes could battle and push back white intruders. In both cases the power of the white settlers and government eventually overcame the Native Americans.)*

NOTE FROM THE AUTHOR
The Indian heritage belongs to all of us. We all can take pride in it. See how many students in your class claim Indian ancestors. Let them talk about their heritage. Suggest that they study and find out more about their ancestry. And if there are no Native Americans in your class? Well, then pretend. Assign Indian ancestry to your students, and have them find out about themselves.

USING THE RUBRICS
To assess these writing assignments, group projects, and activities, scoring rubrics have been provided at the back to this Teaching Guide. Be sure to explain the rubrics to your students.

DEBATING THE ISSUES
Use the topic below to stimulate debate.

Resolved That it was better for the Creek people to learn the ways of the new Americans and become, like them, farmers and traders, than to continue as they did in the past. *(Have opponents take the positions of the Red Sticks and the White Sticks.)*

MAKING ETHICAL JUDGMENTS
The following activity asks students to consider issues of ethics.

Do you believe that non-Indian citizens of the United States had a right to settle land that the United States "owned," even though the land was inhabited by Native Americans? *(Most if not all students probably will argue that the land belonged to the Native Americans. Discuss with the class how attitudes about the right to take land can change over time.)*

PROJECTS AND ACTIVITIES
Writing a Biography The lives of Tecumseh and Osceola are heroic and fascinating. Working in teams, students can research one of these leaders and present a detailed biographical sketch.

Linking Past and Present Working in small groups, students can use the *Readers' Guide to Periodical Literature* to locate articles on the present-day Creek, Seminole, Shawnee, or Iroquois.

Interpreting Figurative Language Native Americans often used images or metaphors in their speeches. Read the first paragraph on page 66 as an example. Figurative language helps listeners form pictures in their minds illustrating the speaker's point. Read the quote from Red Jacket on page 67, and ask students to draw pictures or cartoons based on the metaphor of "the feeble plant" and "mighty tree."

Comparing Maps over Time Have one group of students research and prepare a United States map showing the location of Native American peoples in 1492. Another group should research and prepare a map showing where American Indians live in the United States today. With information from Part 3, students can predict the developments that led to these changes. A resource map showign native American peoples before 1492 is included at the back of this guide.

Giving Dramatic Readings Divide the class into groups to give dramatic readings of Red Jacket's speech on pages 64-66. Encourage students to use body language and hand movements as they speak.

LOOKING AHEAD

Analyzing a Quote

Tell students that in 1811, frustrated and angered that another great piece of Indian land had been taken by the United States, Tecumseh spoke at a gathering of 5,000 in Alabama. He said:

> Let the white race perish. They seize your land; they corrupt your women, they trample on the ashes of your dead! Back whence they came, upon a trail of blood, they must be driven.

Tell students that before he died, Tecumseh joined the British in a war against the United States. Explain that in Part 4 they will learn more about that war.

THE BIG IDEAS

In 1893 the historian Frederick Jackson Turner declared the western frontier "closed" and looked back at this influence on the nation. He wrote:

> To the frontier the American intellect owes its striking characteristics.…[T]hat practical, inventive turn of mind,…that masterful grasp of material things;…that restless, nervous energy, that dominant individualism,…and withal that buoyancy and exuberance which comes with freedom—these are the traits of the frontier.

The Founding Fathers were all from the Eastern Seaboard. Their influence was educated and aristocratic. They had drawn on English and French philosophers for their ideas about democracy. However, the influence of the West began to be felt early in the nineteenth century. It would be a man from the West who would transform the presidency. Eventually, the nation would turn away from Europe and look more to the West for its identity and destiny.

INTRODUCING PART 4

SETTING GOALS

Introduce Part 4 by writing its title, "The Last of the Founding Fathers," on the chalkboard. Discuss the meaning of the term "Founding Fathers." *(The term refers to the men who were involved in writing and ratifying the documents on which our nation and government are based.)* Point out that when the last of these people died, the nation was 50 years old and reaching maturity.

To set goals for Part 4, tell students that they will

- describe the roles and importance of James Madison, James Monroe, John Quincy Adams, and Andrew Jackson.
- trace the events of the War of 1812.
- draw conclusions about a poem on the U.S.S. *Constitution*.
- identify the causes and effects of Florida becoming a state.

SETTING A CONTEXT FOR READING

Thinking About the Big Ideas   On the chalkboard, create a word web around *Americans,* and ask the class to describe the American character. *(rugged individuals, self-made, independent, ambitious, materialistic, puritanical, egalitarian, plain and straightforward, friendly, open, bold, inventive)* Would students describe these characteristics as the identity of the American people? Discuss the idea that although Americans vary as individuals, they collectively present a national character or identity.

Contrasting Eras   Ask students to contrast the U.S. government in 1789, when Washington took office, and 1809, when Jefferson left office. What issues did they have to deal with? *(Washington had to deal with issues of the birth of the nation, such* *as setting up the government, steering clear of foreign problems, and building credibility. Jefferson had to deal with issues of growth: westward expansion, factionalism, how much power the masses should be given, and how the United States should respond to wars in Europe.)*

SETTING A CONTEXT IN SPACE AND TIME

Using Maps   As America expanded, its concept of its regions changed. Have students identify on the map on page 77 the original 13 states, and also the original regions: New England, Middle, South. Then ask them to identify these new states and their regions: Northwest—Ohio, Indiana, Illinois, Michigan; Southwest—Kentucky, Tennessee, Louisiana, Mississippi, Alabama, Missouri. In the first half of the nineteenth century, the latter regions were called the West. Ask students for words describing the West in American history. *(frontier, freedom, and so on)* Tell students to keep this new region in mind as they read Part 4 and to look for the influence of the West on American politics and culture.

Understanding Change over Time   Explain to the class that the next chapters cover the early nineteenth century. Ask what students already know about that time. Explain to the class that the real-life stories in Part 4 will describe the same time period from very different perspectives.

READING NONFICTION

Analyzing Text Structure

Explain that recognizing how an author organizes the text helps readers understand the information better. Help students see that on pages 76 through the top of 78, the organization is main idea and details as the author explains the causes of the War of 1812. From then on, she uses chronological order to describe the course of the war itself.

MORE ABOUT...

The Burning of Washington

Margaret Bayard Smith returned to Washington soon after the British left it, and this is what she saw: "The poor capitol! Nothing but its blacken'd walls remained!...Those beautiful pillars in that Representatives Hall were crack'd and broken, the roof, that noble dome, painted and carved with such beauty and skill, lay in ashes in the cellars beneath the smoldering ruins, were yet smoking."

GEOGRAPHY CONNECTIONS

Battles of the War

Have students create a map of major battles from the War of 1812 on a wall or reproducible map.

CHAPTER 15

THE REVOLUTIONARY WAR PART II, OR THE WAR OF 1812
PAGES 76-83

1 Class Period   Homework: Student Study Guide p. 25

Chapter Summary
War hawks carry the day and the ill-prepared, fledgling nation is drawn into a second war with England.

Key Vocabulary
War Hawks   John Bull   anthem

1. CONNECT

Ask students to describe problems the Americans had had with the English during Washington's and Jefferson's presidencies. *(the refusal of the English to abandon their forts in the Old Northwest, their seizure of American sailors, and interference with American commerce)*

2. UNDERSTAND

1. Read pages 76-78 up to "By that time...." Discuss: How did the generation that included Henry Clay and Andrew Jackson differ from the Founding Fathers' generation? *(The new generation had more hawkish attitudes toward England; and they had not fought in a war.)*
2. Read the rest of the chapter. Discuss: How did the defense of Baltimore at Fort McHenry change the Americans' morale? *(The mood among Americans changed from defeatism to confidence.)*
3. Chart: Have students use Resource Page 6 (TG page 112) to chart the political and economic causes and effects of the War of 1812.

3. CHECK UNDERSTANDING

Writing   Imagine that you are Dolley Madison. Write a diary entry describing the events of 1814 and your part in them.

Thinking About the Chapter (Sequencing)   Have students use a flowchart to trace the sequence of events that led the British to sign another peace treaty with the United States. *(Students should include such events as the burning of Washington, the American victory at Baltimore, the death of the British commander, and other American victories.)*

16 THE OTHER CONSTITUTION

PAGES 84-89

1 Class Period   **Homework: Student Study Guide p. 26**

Chapter Summary

Ordered by President Washington, the U.S.S. *Constitution* was the largest frigate in the world when launched. After a glorious career, she was saved by a poem and is proudly afloat to this day.

Key Vocabulary

Barbary States	corsairs
frigate	bey

1. CONNECT

Ask the class what they know about warships, including the purposes they serve, how they are made, and kinds of weapons they carry. Then ask students to imagine a time when warships were made of wood and powered by the wind.

2. UNDERSTAND

1. Read pages 84-85. Discuss: What made the U.S.S. *Constitution* such a strong ship? *(She was well built, had a hull 25 inches thick with live oak in the center and the best pine for the decks.)*
2. Read the rest of the chapter. Discuss: What are some of the successes that brought fame to the *Constitution*? *(She escaped a British fleet in New York, she destroyed the* Guerrière *in a famous battle and then beat H.M.S.* Java, *she was the flagship at Tripoli in the war against the Barbary pirates, and she helped enforce the ban on slave trading. Schoolchildren raised money to save her, a poem was written about her, and she sails to this day.)*

3. CHECK UNDERSTANDING

Writing   Ask students to write a poem describing the glories of the U.S.S. *Constitution*.

Thinking About the Chapter (Drawing Conclusions)   Engage the class in a discussion of Holmes's poem on page 86. Ask a student to read the poem aloud. Have students conclude what Holmes thinks would be a better fate for the ship. *(that it be allowed to sink in the ocean)* Discuss why Americans of that time would be so affected by the poem. *(To Holmes and many other Americans, the frigate had become a powerful heroic symbol. It was a link to the Revolution. Scrapping the ship would be a "death" too small for the ship's grandeur.)*

MEETING INDIVIDUAL NEEDS

MEETING INDIVIDUAL NEEDS

Interested students might make a glossary of naval jargon that have become common expressions. They can visit the library media center or use the Internet to discover more of these terms. Have them report to the class or make a display on the words, their original nautical meanings, and how they came to be used.

GEOGRAPHY CONNECTIONS

Have students consult the world map in the Atlas in their book. Ask them to locate the Barbary States and to draw conclusions about why the swift-sailing Barbary corsairs were able to control the Mediterranean Sea. (*Access to the Mediterranean is through the narrow strait between Spain and Morocco, where it would be difficult for merchant ships to escape pirates. The Barbary States stretch almost the full length of the Mediterranean.*)

CHAPTER 17

THAT GOOD PRESIDENT MONROE

PAGES 90–92

HISTORY ARCHIVES

A History of US Sourcebook

#33, James Monroe, *The Monroe Doctrine* (1823)

READING NONFICTION

Analyzing Primary and Secondary Sources

Distribute to the class John Quincy Adams' Fourth of July, 1821 Address (Resource Page 10, TG page 116). Have the class read the Address aloud, stopping periodically to clarify the text. Divide them into small groups to discuss and present answers to the questions following the passage.

LINKING DISCIPLINES

Geography/Math

Each degree of latitude is divided into 60 minutes. (Degrees of longitude are also divided this way.) Explain that the latitude in the sidebar on page 91 should be read "36 degrees 30 minutes," which is the equivalent of 36 1/2 degrees. Many almanacs list the latitude and longitude of American cities. Have students find the locations of a number of cities and express them as degrees and minutes and as degrees and fractions of degrees.

MORE ABOUT...

Runaway Slaves in Florida

Florida had long been a haven for enslaved Africans. In the mid-1700s, Fort Mose, a free black community, defended the northern frontier of Florida. The black settlers there vowed to spill their "last drop of blood in defense of the great Crown of Spain and the Holy Faith."

---

1 Class Period   Homework: Student Study Guide p. 27

Chapter Summary

With victory came renewed confidence. The nation turned its back on Europe and looked to its own hemisphere for its identity and destiny.

Key Vocabulary

Monroe Doctrine   expansionist

1. CONNECT

Ask students to summarize what they know about the Founding Fathers. *(These men who helped start the nation were wealthy, well educated, and felt that it was their duty to serve their country.)*

2. UNDERSTAND

1. Read pages 90-92 up to "Some Americans were upset." Discuss: Why would Southern planters be especially interested in gaining Florida from Spain? *(As long as Florida remained Spanish, enslaved people could escape and be free there.)*
2. Read the rest of the chapter. Discuss: What events led to the Monroe Doctrine? *(the weakening of Spain, a wave of revolutions in Central and South America, and fear among Americans that other European nations might try to gain power in Latin America)*
3. Time Line: Have students use Resource Page 7 (TG page 113) to plot the foreign policy of Madison and Monroe.

3. CHECK UNDERSTANDING

Writing   Have students write a one-paragraph description of James Monroe and his presidency.

Thinking About the Chapter (Identifying Cause and Effect)
Have the class discuss the causes and effects of Florida becoming part of the United States. Begin by asking students to explain why Jackson invaded Florida. *(He was sent there to capture people who had fled enslavement in the United States.)* Then ask students to discuss the effect of Jackson's invasion. *(Although the invasion was not right, Spain was too weak to defend her colony, and agreed to sell it when the United States offered $5 million.)*

CHAPTER 18 · JQA VS. AJ

PAGES 76-83

1 Class Period   Homework: Student Study Guide p. 28

Chapter Summary
After 24 years of Democratic-Republican rule, new interests and parties began to vie for power. At the same time, the West emerged as a political force.

Key Vocabulary
diplomat

1. CONNECT

Ask students to describe what they already know about John Quincy Adams and his family. (You may wish to take a look back at Chapter 7.)

2. UNDERSTAND

1. Read pages 93-94. Discuss: What kind of person was John Quincy Adams? Why does the author call his term as president "the era of political grouchiness"? (*Adams's personal qualities—puritanical, educated, honest, virtuous, serious—did not create a happy or lively political climate.*)
2. Read the rest of the chapter. Discuss: When Elijah Fletcher left New England and went south, what differences did he note? (*He saw many log cabins and stone buildings. New Jersey was undeveloped. Property in Virginia was unequally distributed; he saw a few mansions and many very poor homes.*)

3. CHECK UNDERSTANDING

Writing   Ask students to write a paragraph describing the presidency of John Quincy Adams.

Thinking About the Chapter (Evaluating)   Have students describe what conditions would be called "political grouchiness." (*arguments over policy, divided Congress, bad feelings between parties, and so on*) Ask them to evaluate how much of this could be attributed to Adams's personality and how much could be attributed to the changing balance of political power (the rise of the West).

READING NONFICTION
Analyzing Primary and Secondary Sources
Before reading the chapter, have partners read the letter written by John Quincy Adams on page 93 and use it to list the boy's character traits. (*respectful, intelligent, formal, and so on*) Then have students read the first two paragraphs of the chapter, and analyze how the primary source supports the author's claim that Adams was "honest, intelligent, virtuous, and hardworking."

MORE ABOUT...
Before the Secret Service
Use the following excerpt from Adams's diary to demonstrate how the life of a president has changed since the early 1800s. "Swam with Antoine [a servant] an hour in the Potomac [River]...but after swimming about half an hour, I perceived...that we had ascended very little above where we had left our clothes, and that the current...was...carrying us into the middle of the river. We continued struggling...about twenty minutes longer....I then turned back, and...landed at the rock where I had left my clothes." Ask students to imagine how the event would be different today. (*Today presidents are heavily guarded by the Secret Service and can't move about freely.*)

Recent immigrants might benefit from completing a research project on the various ways Americans celebrate the Fourth of July. Have students develop and use a questionnaire to find out what Americans typically do to celebrate Independence Day. Students might also compare the American Independence Day to similar holidays in their countries of origin.

CHAPTER 19 | A DAY OF CELEBRATION AND TEARS

PAGES 96-98

1 Class Period   **Homework: Student Study Guide p. 29**

Chapter Summary
The deaths of Thomas Jefferson and John Adams on the nation's 50th birthday marked the end of an era.

Key Vocabulary
creed

1. CONNECT

Ask students to describe what they know about the Fourth of July, including typical celebrations and the date's significance.

2. UNDERSTAND

1. Read pages 96-97. Discuss: Why were people from other countries "pouring into America"? *(They wanted to live in a nation where they were guaranteed the right to life, liberty, and the pursuit of happiness.)*
2. Read the rest of the chapter. Discuss: How were Adams's and Jefferson's statements typical of their personalities? *(Adams warned that the future could be bright or dark, depending on the people; Jefferson was concerned with human rights and equality and the extension of liberty as well as science.)*

3. CHECK UNDERSTANDING

Writing   Ask students to imagine that they are newspaper reporters in 1826. Have them write a front-page story about the nation's 50th Independence Day.

Thinking About the Chapter (Drawing Conclusions)   Elicit that the lives of Adams and Jefferson encompassed the nation's birth and growth into a strong country, and that without these two the United States might be a very different nation. Have students make a chart on the chalkboard listing each man's contributions to the governmental, political, and economic development of the nation. Lead students to the conclusion that the interplay of these two and their supporters truly shaped the United States.

CHAPTER 20 · OLD HICKORY

PAGES 99–102

1 Class Period   **Homework: Student Study Guide p. 30**

Chapter Summary

The election of Andrew Jackson—the first president who was not an Eastern aristocrat—set a precedent for government *by* the people.

Key Vocabulary

Old Hickory   spoils system

1. CONNECT

Ask a student to read the The Last Battle feature on page 82, and have students discuss what they already know about Andrew Jackson.

2. UNDERSTAND

1. Read pages 99-101 up to "But when Harvard...." Discuss: How did Jackson differ from the previous presidents? *(The other presidents were all wealthy, educated aristocrats from Massachusetts or Virginia who played important roles in the birth of the nation. Jackson was from the West, had little formal education, was a youth during the Revolution, and was a leader of the common people.)*
2. Read the rest of the chapter. Discuss: What did Federalists and Democratic-Republicans think about the Jacksonian Democrats? *(They thought Jackson's supporters were a mob that would destroy the United States.)* Why didn't this happen? *(Jackson was a great leader who made the government* by *the people as well as* for *the people.)*
3. Map: Have students complete Resource Page 8 (TG page 120) to answer questions about the 1828 election and the formation of the Democratic Party.

3. CHECK UNDERSTANDING

Writing   Have students imagine that they are Jackson supporters who have just attended Jackson's inauguration. Ask them to write diary entries about the experience.

Thinking About the Chapter (Analyzing)   Jackson's motto was, "Let the people rule." Have students list Jackson's life experiences that would have solidified this belief for him. *(Students should list details about his life among the common people of the frontier and in the army. They should recognize how such experiences would give him faith in the intelligence and common sense of the people.)*

JOHNS HOPKINS TEAM LEARNING

WHAT AN INAUGURATION!

1 EXTENDED CLASS PERIOD

FOCUS ACTIVITY

1. Organize students into teams of four. Have teams **Brainstorm** what they know about modern inaugurations. Encourage teams to list specific details about recent presidential inaugurations, including speeches, poems, and balls.

2. Have teams use **Roundtable** to create a word web describing Andrew Jackson's inauguration.

3. Explain that in the upcoming activity, teams will use first-hand descriptions of Jackson's inauguration to create a political cartoon about the event.

STUDENT TEAM LEARNING ACTIVITY/USING PRIMARY SOURCES TO CREATE POLITICAL CARTOONS

1. Read the following first-hand accounts of Jackson's inauguration to the class. Read them a second time while teams take notes.

> *Yesterday the President's house was open at noon....The old man stood in the center of the little circle...and shook hands with anybody that offered....There was a throng of apprentices, boys of all ages, men not civilized enough to walk about the rooms with their hats off; the vilest...[group] that ever [gathered] in a decent house; many of the lowest gathering around the door, pouncing...upon the...refreshments, tearing the cake...all fellows with dirty faces and dirty manners; all the [trash] that Washington could turn forth from its workshops and stables.*
>
> *George Bancroft's*
> *1831 White House Inaugural Description*

> *A rabble, a mob, of boys, negros, women, children, scrambling, fighting, romping. What a pity what a pity! No arrangement had been made, no police officers on duty, and the whole house had been [filled] by the rabble mob.*
> *Unknown Jackson inaugural party witness*

2. Tell teams to discuss what the descriptions say about democracy during the Jackson presidency, and whether such access to the government was positive or negative for the country.

3. Divide teams into partnerships, and ask each pair of students to draw a political cartoon about Jackson's inaugural party based on the first-person descriptions.

4. Sharing Information When finished, each partnership should share its cartoon with the rest of the team and explain its point of view about democracy under Jackson.

5. Circulate and Monitor As partnerships work, systematically visit them. If they need help, refer students to the political cartoons on pages 93 and 100.

6. Have the class create a display of their cartoons. Discuss: How does Jackson's accessibility contrast with the present? Is this difference good or bad for our democracy?

ASSESSMENT

Part 4 Check-Up Use Check-Up 4 (TG page 103) to assess student learning in Part 4.

ALTERNATE ASSESSMENT
Ask students to write an essay answering one of the following questions, which link the big ideas across chapters:

1. Making Connections How did each of the following change how Americans felt about themselves: the Battle of New Orleans, the War of 1812, the Monroe Doctrine, the election of Andrew Jackson? *(The Battle of New Orleans made them proud. The War of 1812 made them confident and more independent. The Monroe Doctrine drew them closer to their neighbors. The election of Jackson gave them confidence in the common man.)*

2. Making Connections During the early nineteenth century, Americans were so proud and confident that they felt they could conquer the world. What events contributed to this feeling? *(They had beaten the British twice, gained political and economic independence, expanded into new regions, and extended democracy to more people than ever before.)*

DEBATING THE ISSUES
Use the topic below to stimulate debate.

Resolved That the War of 1812 was unavoidable. (Have a panel discussion, with students role-playing War Hawks from the West, such as Henry Clay and Andrew Jackson; New Englanders opposed to the war because it would threaten their overseas trade; pro-England and anti-France speakers; and a military expert to speak on the level of American preparedness for war against England.)

MAKING ETHICAL JUDGMENTS
The following activity asks students to consider issues of ethics.

When Harvard University gave Andrew Jackson an honorary degree, John Quincy Adams was so horrified that he refused to attend the ceremony. Write a letter from Adams to the president of Harvard explaining his views. Then write a reply from the president of Harvard defending his decision.

PROJECTS AND ACTIVITIES
Researching the Flag Have students research the history of the American flag. They should draw examples of their findings and make a display, including the proper way to display and care for the flag.

SUMMARIZING PART 4

NOTE FROM THE AUTHOR

Have each of your students choose a picture in this book and write about it. Suggest that they do two papers: one imaginative, the other based on some research. Send them to the library to find out more about the subject of the picture.

USING THE RUBRICS

To assess these writing assignments, group projects, and activities, scoring rubrics have been provided at the back to this Teaching Guide. Be sure to explain the rubrics to your students.

LOOKING AHEAD

Interpreting a Primary Source

Tell students that a new sound was about to be heard in the nation. It was the hum of machines and songs about workers. This one is about the women who worked at the mills.

She tends the loom, she watches the spindle,
And cheerfully talketh away;
Mid the din of wheels, how her bright eyes
kindle!

Ask: What kind of scene does the song describe? Does the song make the work sound like fun? Explain that young women and girls sometimes worked in the mills for fourteen hours a day for one dollar a week with board. Would the real workers think the work cheerful? Tell students that in Part 5 they will learn about another revolution—the Industrial Revolution—and the whirlwind of change it began.

Drawing Political Cartoons   Tell students that the first time "Uncle Sam" was used to represent the United States in a cartoon was during the War of 1812. Since then thousands of cartoonists have drawn the tall man in striped pants and a top hat. Ask students to draw a political cartoon about an issued discussed in this part that includes Uncle Sam. Possible topics are the Monroe Doctrine, the War of 1812, or the nation's 50th birthday.

Writing Letters   Have pairs of students imagine they are Jefferson and Adams in retirement, and write each other letters. Remind students that both men would be very knowledgeable about current events and how they relate to their shared past. Have pairs read their letters to the class.

Writing Patriotic Verse   Remind students how Francis Scott Key's lyrics inspired the nation and helped to win the War of 1812. Ask them to think of the drama of the defense of Baltimore. If Americans had lost that city, they might well have lost the war. With that in mind, have students write patriotic poems or songs about the defense of Baltimore.

Comparing Regions   Ask students to select the North, the South, or the West for further investigation. Students should do further research on the Internet or in the library media center in order to write a detailed description of a typical day in the life of a person their age from that region in the early 1800s. Have students share their reports with the class.

THE BIG IDEAS

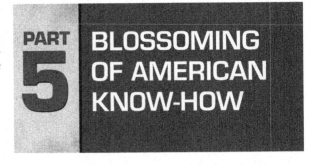

I n 1814, Nathan Appleton watched as inventor Francis Lowell started up the first mechanized loom to run in America. He later wrote:

I well recollect the state of admiration and satisfaction with which we sat by the hour watching the beautiful movement of this new and wonderful machine.

What Nathan Appleton and Francis Lowell witnessed was the birth of the Industrial Revolution in America. This revolution would transform the jobs, the tools, and the lives of every person in the United States.

INTRODUCING PART 5

SETTING GOALS

Introduce Part 5 by writing its title, "Blossoming of American Know-How," on the chalkboard. Ask students what "know-how" the title might be referring to. Have the class skim the artwork on pages 103-123 to find out. *(Industrial and technological innovations are pictured.)*

To set goals for Part 5, tell students that they will
- describe the roles and importance of Samuel Slater, Francis Cabot Lowell, Eli Whitney, DeWitt Clinton, Robert Fulton, and Peter Cooper.
- make judgments about the benefits and drawbacks of the Industrial Revolution.
- describe the great expansion of railroads from 1830 to 1850.

SETTING A CONTEXT FOR READING

Thinking About the Big Ideas   Read aloud the words of Gordon Wood in the sidebar on page 103. Have students explore what a people needs to make such a transition. *(stable government, abundant natural resources, adequate labor supply, technology, security)* Discuss the importance of America's isolation. Because no greater power threatened the nation's independence, Americans could turn their attentions to internal development.

Visualizing   Ask students to visualize the American landscape in 1829 when Andrew Jackson was inaugurated. What would an observer see in the North, South, and West. *(Possible responses: farms, villages, forests, dirt roads, a few cities along the coast)* Remind students to visualize how the landscape was changing as they read Part 5.

SETTING A CONTEXT IN SPACE AND TIME

Linking Geography and Identity   Explain that regional identities were beginning to shift. By the 1800s, New England and the Middle States were increasingly referred to as "the North." Ask: What other identity shifts were occurring? (Parts of the old Northwest and Southwest territories were known as the West, and the other parts of those territories became identified with the South and the North.) Ask students to watch for evidence of these new regional divisions as they read.

To assess these writing assignments, group projects, and activities, scoring rubrics have been provided at the back to this Teaching Guide. Be sure to explain the rubrics to your students.

Understanding Change over Time Explain to students that in Chapters 21-23, they will read about more "firsts"—in inventions and technology. Discuss how one advance often leads to others. In the 1800s, a few inventions led to so many others that the period became known as the Industrial Revolution. Help students decide how best to show this period on a time line. One solution would be to indicate the Industrial Revolution on the class time line, and then have mini-time lines showing related developments.

21 YANKEE INGENUITY: COTTON AND MUSKETS
PAGES 103-109

1 Class Period   **Homework: Student Study Guide p. 31**

Chapter Summary
England closely guarded its industrial secrets but American opportunity lured them across the Atlantic.

Key Vocabulary
Industrial Revolution   cotton gin
market revolution   farm economy
market economy   interchangeable parts

1. CONNECT

Ask students if they have ever seen a typewriter being used. Discuss why typewriters are almost obsolete. *(Computers have replaced them.)* Have students describe what they know about the era before machines like typewriters, light bulbs, or steam engines were invented.

2. UNDERSTAND

1. Read pages 103-105. Discuss: Why are the industrial changes in the early 1800s called a revolution? *(The changes were so far-reaching that they radically altered—or caused a revolution in—how people lived and worked and how society operated.)*
2. Read the rest of the chapter. Discuss: Compare and contrast the way of life of people in a self-sufficient farm economy with that of workers in a capitalist market economy. *(In the farm economy, people meet their own needs; money is rarely used. In the market economy, people sell their labor for wages, which are exchanged to meet their needs; people are more interdependent.)*

3. CHECK UNDERSTANDING

Writing Ask students to imagine that they are Virginian newspaper reporters visiting Massachusetts. Have them write a one-paragraph article about the Industrial Revolution there.

Thinking About the Chapter (Making Judgments) Have students discuss how the Industrial Revolution transformed the landscape, how people worked, and how they obtained goods. Ask what the benefits and the drawbacks of those changes were. *(Benefits included affordable goods and interchangeable parts. Drawbacks included pollution, child labor, poor working conditions, and, in the South, a more firmly entrenched system of slavery.)*

MORE ABOUT...

Lowell Bells
Lucy Larcom and all the factory workers in Lowell lived according to the mill bells. The bells rang out at 5:40 A.M. to wake everyone up, at 6:00 to get them to work, at 7:30 for breakfast, at 12:30 P.M. for lunch, at 7:30 when work was done, and finally at 10:00 for bedtime!

MEETING INDIVIDUAL NEEDS

Have students research some of the machines first used during the Industrial Revolution, such as the power loom or cotton gin. Ask them to find out how a particular machine operated. Suggest that students draw a labeled diagram of the machine and explain to the class how it operated.

See the Student Team Learning Activity on TG page 72.

MORE ABOUT...

The Erie Canal

A speed limit of 4 miles per hour was set for the canal boats. Boats moving any faster than that created waves, and waves caused erosion. The boats also had to be raised or lowered 565 feet by a series of 83 locks. In addition, the horses or mules had to be changed or rested. The best time a boat could make was 80 miles in 24 hours. At that speed it took four and a half days to travel the length of the canal—much faster than before the canal.

LINKING DISCIPLINES

History/Math

The total cost of building the Erie Canal was $7 million, and the length was 360 miles. Challenge your students to find the cost per mile and per foot to construct the canal. (*approximately $19,444 per mile; approximately $3.68 per foot*)

CHAPTER 22 GOING PLACES

1 Class Period   Homework: Student Study Guide p. 32

Chapter Summary

Raw materials were in the South and the West; the North needed them. Surplus goods piled up around the factories; the South and the West wanted them. Nothing less than a transportation revolution could meet the need caused by the Industrial Revolution.

Key Vocabulary

corduroy	macadam	pike
lock	celeripede	aqueduct

1. CONNECT

Ask students to describe what transportation was like before cars, motor boats, and jets existed. Have them imagine how people traveled and how people shipped heavy items: a load of coal, a bale of cotton, or a side of beef. (*People walked or rode horses. Coal and cotton: hauled by horses to water; loaded onto wind-powered boats. Cattle: walked to market and slaughtered there.*)

2. UNDERSTAND

1. Read pages 110-112. Discuss: Why did building the National Road stir up regional differences? (*The road was of the greatest benefit to the western states, so they supported it. People in the South and the East questioned whether they should have to pay for something they didn't believe would benefit them directly.*) Have students discuss whether all parts of a nation benefit when one region is helped.
2. Read the rest of the chapter. Ask: What were the effects of the Erie Canal? (*lowered the cost of transportation and shipping; it caused towns to develop along its route; resulted in New York City becoming the nation's largest city; opened Indiana, Michigan, and Wisconsin to settlers*)

3. CHECK UNDERSTANDING

Writing Ask students to pretend that they are Benjamin Franklin and can travel through time to witness the Industrial Revolution. Have them write one paragraph describing some of the inventions that would particularly interest him.

Thinking About the Chapter (Comparing and Contrasting) Have the class discuss differences in getting goods to market before and after the Industrial Revolution. (*Before: Transportation was slow, difficult, and expensive. After: Roads improved and bridges, aqueducts, and canals were built, so goods could be moved greater distances more quickly and cheaply.*)

23 TEAKETTLE POWER

PAGES 117–123

1 Class Period Homework: Student Study Guide p. 33

Chapter Summary

Water power ran the mills, but it could not power means of transportation. English and American inventors tinkered with steam power. Soon steamships plied the rivers and railroads crossed the land.

Key Vocabulary

iron horses   locomotives
steam power   horsepower

1. CONNECT

Ask the students to describe what they already know about teakettles and the power of steam.

2. UNDERSTAND

1. Read pages 117-120 up to "*Tom Thumb* worried a Baltimore stagecoach company." Explain: Fulton's steamboat was called Fulton's Folly by skeptical viewers. Ask: What essential quality did inventors Fulton and Cooper have? *(They both stubbornly refused to believe anyone who said "it can't be done.")*

2. Read the rest of the chapter. Discuss: What were some of the benefits and drawbacks of steam-powered trains? *(Benefits: They were fast, could run in winter when canals and rivers froze, and could pull great weights. Drawbacks: They could have explosions, fires, and train wrecks.)*

3. Map: Have students turn to the map of major transportation routes in 1840 on pages 122-123. Ask students to identify the region with the most canals and railroads. *(the North).* Discuss why most trails in the far Southwest linked the region with Mexican communities. *(Much of the far Southwest was part of Mexico.)*

3. CHECK UNDERSTANDING

Writing Ask students to write a paragraph describing the highlights of America's transportation revolution.

Thinking About the Chapter (Sequencing) Engage the class in a discussion of the growth of railroads. Have them identify how many miles of track there were in 1830, 1840, 1850, and 1860. Then ask students to use the information to make a bar graph. *(Miles of track: 1830—13 miles, 1840—3,000 miles, 1850—9,000 miles, 1860—30,000 miles)* Have them perform a similar activity for the growth of steamboats on the Mississippi River. *(1820— 60 steamboats; 1860—1,000 steamboats)*

READING NONFICTION

Analyzing Graphic Aids

Have students describe the elements of the cartoon on page 121. (*It is one drawing without any text.*) Have students contrast this cartoon with the political cartoons on pages 79 and 93. (*The earlier cartoons use multiple images and a lot of text*). Which type of cartoon is more like the ones we see on today's editorial pages? Why? (*The teakettle cartoon is more like modern-day political cartoons, because it relies solely on a strong visual for impact.*)

LINKING DISCIPLINES

History/Math

On page 117, the author asks students to calculate the Clermont's speed (*about 4.7 miles per hour*). Have students use that figure and the following ones to create a bar graph showing speeds of transportation in the early 1800s: Walking—about 3 miles per hour; horse-drawn wagon—about 4 miles per hour; horse and rider—about 9 miles per hour; Tom Thumb steam engine—about 13 miles per hour.

JOHNS HOPKINS TEAM LEARNING

TRAVELING ALONG THE NATIONAL ROAD

2 EXTENDED CLASS PERIODS

FOCUS ACTIVITY

1. Divide the class into teams of four students each. Have teams use **Think-Team-Share** to describe a recent trip they have taken.

2. Have teams ask these questions about each member's trip: Where did you travel? How did you travel? How much time did it take to get there? How many miles away was your destination? What did you enjoy most about the trip?

STUDENT TEAM LEARNING ACTIVITY/RESEARCHING AND DISPLAYING INFORMATION

1. Explain to teams that they will be researching the National Road in order to create a travel brochure for a trip from Baltimore, Maryland, to Vandalia, Illinois, in the 1830s. Have teams **Brainstorm** ways to research the National Road at the library media center. Remind them that they can use Book Four as well as reference sources such as encyclopedias, history books, and the Internet. (An excellent source about the Mount Washington Tavern, ca. 1820, in Farmington, Pennsylvania, is *www.nps.gov/fone/mwt.htm*.)

2. Divide each team into two partnerships, and have students **Partner Read** Chapter 22 to review details about the National Road. Then have each partnership do further research on the National Road at the library media center.

3. When students are finished researching, help them design their brochures. Suggest that they consider the towns to be visited along the way, the toll booths on the route, any historical or commercial sites of interest, travel comfort, the modes of transportation available, and accommodations along the way. Partners should illustrate their brochures with small maps and drawings of the means of transportation and accommodations.

4. Sharing Information When each partnership is finished, have them share their brochures with their teammates. Ask teams to use the brochures to compare transportation then and now in terms of, speed, expense, comfort, and safety.

5. Circulate and Monitor As partners work on their brochures, systematically visit them. If necessary, help students locate information about the National Road. Explain that the National Road later became U.S. Route 40, which is still a major highway.

6. Have students create a class display of their brochures.

ASSESSMENT

Part 5 Check-Up   Use Check-Up 5 (TG page 104) to assess student learning in Part 5.

ALTERNATE ASSESSMENT

Ask students to write an essay answering one of the following questions, which link the big ideas across chapters:

1. Making Connections   How did the Industrial Revolution lead to the development of modern transportation? *(Because of the Industrial Revolution, there was a greater demand for transportation to ship goods and raw materials; new technologies and means of transportation were developed, such as steam engines, canals, and better roads in response to this need.)*

2. Making Connections   Did the Industrial Revolution increase or decrease the differences between the North and the South? *(It increased the differences between the regions because it made the North more urban and industrial and kept the South rural and agricultural.)*

DEBATING THE ISSUES

Use the topic below to stimulate debate.

Resolved   That to rid society of poverty and to instruct foreign children in American principles, it is to everybody's best interest to employ children in factories and mills. (To provoke debate, appoint students to argue as mill owners, as children, and as parents.)

MAKING ETHICAL JUDGMENTS

The following activity asks students to consider issues of ethics.

Eli Whitney's invention sealed the fate of generations of Southern blacks. Should Eli Whitney have thought about these effects of his cotton gin? Are inventors responsible for the long-range results of their work? This is a hard question that bothers many scientists today. Explain how you feel about this question. *(Students' responses should reflect the complexities of this issue.)*

PROJECTS AND ACTIVITIES

Exploring Etymology   Tell students that inventions often bring new words into the language. For example, before bicycles were invented, there was no such word. Ask students to search for and list examples of English words that might have come from the Industrial Revolution. *(Students may suggest railroad, cotton gin, industrial revolution, macadam road, piker, steamboat, submarine, and steam engine.)* To extend this activity, have students list some of the words that have come into usage today because of computers.

NOTE FROM THE AUTHOR

I love to add new words to my vocabulary, especially words that are fine-sounding. It makes me feel important and smart. I don't think I'm alone in that feeling. Put out a sign-up sheet, and ask each of your students to pick a word from this book. Then have them report back to the class on their words—not just their meaning, but also their derivation. What is the story of the word?

USING THE RUBRICS

To assess these writing assignments, group projects, and activities, scoring rubrics have been provided at the back to this Teaching Guide. Be sure to explain the rubrics to your students.

LOOKING AHEAD

Interpreting a Quotation

Tell students that because the cotton gin encouraged the cotton economy in the South, it caused a vast "land grab." The land that whites grabbed had previously been home to the Cherokee, Choctaw, Chickasaw, Creek, and Seminole peoples. The Cherokee Nation made a public plea for justice, which said, in part:

> We are aware that some persons suppose it will be for our advantage to remove beyond the Mississippi. We think otherwise....We wish to remain on the land of our fathers. We have a perfect and original right to remain.

Ask: What did the Cherokee people want? What claims did they have to the land? Tell students that out of this conflict, new voices for freedom would be heard. The lives of these freedom fighters will form the subject of Part 6.

Using Historical Imagination   Have students work in pairs or small groups to imagine that they are passengers on the *Clermont* or the *Tom Thumb*. Suggest that they present to the class short plays about their adventure.

Writing a Play   Have students imagine a conversation between James Armistead Lafayette and the Marquis Lafayette when they met again in 1824. Have them write a short dialogue about what the two men said to each other.

Rereading and Writing Diaries   Ask students to imagine they are poor immigrants just arrived in America without jobs or homes. Write diary entries about their impressions of the United States.

THE BIG IDEAS

In 1830, both popular opinion and President Jackson were for the removal of Native Americans from the newly formed states in the West. The president gave this message to Congress in 1830:

> It gives me pleasure to announce to Congress...[that] the removal of the Indians beyond the white settlements is approaching to a happy consummation...It will relieve the whole state of Mississippi and the western part of Alabama of Indian occupancy, and enable those states to advance rapidly in population, wealth, and power.

Under Jackson's leadership, America rushed headlong on its expansionist course. Taking advantage of new opportunities, the population and settlements of the West and the cotton/slave empire of the South developed at an unprecedented rate. Part 6 describes the cost of this growth to Native Americans and African-Americans.

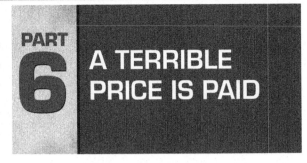

PART 6

A TERRIBLE PRICE IS PAID

INTRODUCING PART 6

SETTING GOALS

Introduce Part 6 by writing its title, "A Terrible Price Is Paid," on the chalkboard. Ask students to flip through pages 124-152 and look at the pictures to help them answer the question Who paid a terrible price? *(Students should note that both Native Americans and African-Americans paid a terrible price as the nation grew and developed.)*

To set goals for Part 6, tell students that they will
- describe the roles and importance of Sequoyah, Andrew Jackson, Justice John Marshall, Osceola, Paul Cuffe, Robert Carter III, and Elizabeth Freeman.
- evaluate the reasons people gave for removing Indians from their lands in the East.
- summarize Justice John Marshall's decision on the proposed removal of the Cherokee people.
- create a sequence diagram to show the escalating military campaigns against the Seminoles.

SETTING A CONTEXT FOR READING

Thinking About the Big Ideas   You can link the ideas of expansion with conflict and questions of human rights by asking: How do nations grow? Lead students to realize that because the earth is a finite space, the growth of one nation is often at the expense of another. Remind students that the cotton gin caused the South to grow. Ask: As the South grew, who was squeezed out? *(the Indians)* Read aloud the quote by Andrew Jackson above. Ask: Whose point of view does this express? *(white Americans')* How would the Indians' point of view have differed? *(Obviously, they would have disagreed with this point of view because they wanted to keep their lands.)*

Evaluating Credibility of a Source   As students read Part 6, they will encounter many views by and about Native Americans and African-Americans. Discuss the prejudices that might have grown among other people (such as white settlers and European immigrants) toward these groups. Ask students to carefully evaluate the credibility of each primary source as they read Part 6, and to look for evidence of the prejudices that were so common at that time.

SETTING A CONTEXT IN SPACE AND TIME

Using Maps   Ask students to turn to the map on page 128. Remind them that the frontier was constantly moving west as the flow of settlers crossing the Appalachian Mountains grew from a trickle to a flood in the early 1800s. Ask students to use information on the map to decide where the frontier might be during the period 1825-1850. *(much farther west, in the region of the Indian Territory)* Explain that while the North became more industrialized, the South also went through profound changes. In time, the South would extend from the southern Appalachian Mountains almost to central Texas.

Map Activity   In Part 6, students will read about the displacement of Native Americans. Have them track locations and routes on a wall or reproducible map. A blank map for this activity is found in this guide.

Understanding Change over Time   Tell students that the chapters in Part 6 cover events in the lives of Native Americans and African-Americans in the first half of the 1800s. Have them use the Chronology of Events on page 181 to note entries about these two groups of Americans.

HISTORY ARCHIVES

A History of US Sourcebook
#34, From *Memorial of the Cherokee Nation*
(1830)

1 Class Period   Homework: Student Study Guide p. 34

Chapter Summary
Many Cherokees adapted to white ways and prospered. But still they could not save their homelands.

Key Vocabulary
Indian Removal Act

1. CONNECT

Ask students to describe what they already know about the population in the West, the region that stretched between the Appalachian Mountains and the Mississippi River. Have them explain who lived there. *(Native Americans lived there, but many settlers were streaming in.)*

2. UNDERSTAND

1. Read pages 124-126. Discuss: What does Sequoyah's life story tell you about him and the Cherokee people? *(It reveals that he and his people were proud, determined, and willing to change if change proved worthy.)*
2. Read the rest of the chapter. Discuss: Where were the Cherokee homelands, and why did immigrants and others want those lands for themselves? *(Cherokee homelands comprised the southern Appalachian foothills from Kentucky to Alabama; immigrants wanted the fertile land and fresh water. Soon others came in search of gold.)*
3. Map: Have students color in the area on Resource Page 5 (TG page 97) that was once home to the Cherokee people. *(Kentucky and Tennessee except for the far western tips; the northern tip of Alabama and Georgia; and the western edge of Virginia, North Carolina, and South Carolina.)* Then have them turn to the Resource Map in the Atlas in their books to find where gold was discovered on Cherokee land, and add that to their map and key.

3. CHECK UNDERSTANDING

Writing   Ask students to write a one-paragraph biography of Sequoyah.

Thinking About the Chapter (Evaluating)   Have the class evaluate the reasons people gave for removing Native Americans from their lands in 1830. Then have students evaluate the author's descriptions of the true causes for their removal *(People said that the Indians would be safe and could live in peace beyond the Mississippi, but the author says the real cause for their removal was greed.)*

READING NONFICTION

Analyzing Rhetorical Devices

Tell students that writers may attempt to persuade readers of their point of view by making appeals that convince by their logic or that stir emotions and touch a sympathetic chord in the reader. Ask: In the first paragraph on page 129, what technique does the author use? (*emotional appeal*) Which words produce emotional responses? (*wept, homes, mothers, fathers*).

LINKING DISCIPLINES

History/Genealogy

For students who are interested in tracing their own family trees, suggest that they find out about their roots. In African-American communities, it is fairly common to find families with ancestors who are Choctaw, Creek, Chickasaw, or Cherokee. Encourage students to learn what they can about their ancestors and share their findings with the class.

MORE ABOUT...

The Cherokee

Today the Cherokee nation includes the Eastern Cherokee, who live in the mountains of North Carolina, and the Western Cherokee of Oklahoma.

CHAPTER 25 | A TIME TO WEEP

PAGES 129–133

1 Class Period   Homework: Student Study Guide p. 35

Chapter Summary

Contrary to Indians' wishes and U.S. law, one Indian nation after another was moved west. Andrew Jackson, with popular opinion behind him, ruled the day.

Key Vocabulary

Trail of Tears

1. CONNECT

Ask students to describe what it is like to move to an unfamiliar place. Have students discuss what people have to leave behind. (*familiar or favorite people and places, a climate they are used to, and holidays or other cultural events that they shared with family and friends*) Now ask students to imagine how they would feel if they were forced to move from their homes.

2. UNDERSTAND

1. Read the main text on pages 129-133. Discuss: Why is *Worcester* v. *Georgia* an important case? (*The Cherokee won the right to their own land, even though President Jackson disobeyed the Court. Today the case is often cited in human rights disputes.*)
2. Ask students: What was John Marshall's position in *Worcester* v. *Georgia*? (*Marshall argued that the Cherokee nation was a distinct community and that the laws of the state of Georgia had no authority over it.*)

3. CHECK UNDERSTANDING

Writing   Ask students to imagine that they are reporters covering the Trail of Tears. Ask them to write a brief newspaper article about the events surrounding the removal of the Cherokee.

Thinking About the Chapter (Analyzing)   Have students read the *Barron* v. *Baltimore* feature on pages 132–133. Ask them to discuss the significance of Congress's passage of the 14th amendment as a response to Justice Marshall's judicial review of the case. (*Marshall, who was trying to prevent the federal government from becoming too powerful, ruled that the federal government could not protect citizens from state laws. The 14th amendment declared otherwise: it said that no state could make laws that deprived "any person of life, liberty, or property without due process of law." Congress, by passing the 14th amendment, rejected Marshall's view.*)

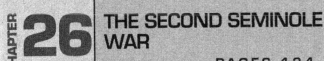

CHAPTER 26 | THE SECOND SEMINOLE WAR

PAGES 134-137

1 Class Period   Homework: Student Study Guide p. 36

Chapter Summary
As Americans pushed south, the Seminoles stood their ground. The great warrior chief Osceola led the Seminoles in a bitter war of resistance.

Key Vocabulary
homesteaders   guerrilla bands

1. CONNECT

Ask the class what they already know about Osceola and the Seminole Indians of Florida. Have them review Chapter 14 (pages 73-75) to refresh their memories.

2. UNDERSTAND

1. Read pages 134-135 up to "Major Francis L. Dade marched to Florida...." Discuss: What factors contributed to the Seminoles' decision to resist removal? *(The Seminoles refused to move when they found that their new home would be with their Creek enemies, the White Sticks, and that the government would not protect them from the White Sticks.)*
2. Read the rest of the chapter. Discuss: How were the Seminoles finally defeated? *(First, both sides grew tired of fighting, and Osceola caught malaria. Then soldiers tricked the Seminoles and captured Osceola. After Osceola died in prison, most Seminoles gave up.)*

3. CHECK UNDERSTANDING

Writing   Have students write a one-paragraph description of Osceola's traits as a leader.

Thinking About the Chapter (Sequencing)   Engage the class in a discussion of the escalating military campaigns against the Seminoles. Then have the class create a sequence diagram of the campaigns. *(Students should note the campaigns of Major Francis L. Dade with two companies of troops; General Duncan Clinch with a large army; General Edmund P. Gaines with a bigger force; General Winfield Scott with an even larger army; General Robert Call; Bloodhounds that were brought from Cuba; and General Thomas S. Jesup with the largest army yet.)*

GEOGRAPHY CONNECTIONS
Discuss with students how Florida's geography helped the Seminoles resist so many U.S. soldiers for so long. (*Students may mention swamps where the Seminoles could hide, the hot climate, and disease.*)

NOTE FROM THE AUTHOR
For most of our national history, the Indian peoples didn't seem to have any "unalienable rights." Their fierce resistance to subjugation led to Indian-bashing that was both physical and psychological. Those humiliations and hurts are finally being seen for what they are: a national disgrace.

ACTIVITIES/ JOHNS HOPKINS TEAM LEARNING
See the Student Team Learning Activity on TG page 84.

READING NONFICTION

Analyzing Word Choice

Ask partners to list the antonyms the author uses on page 138 to explain the paradoxes in American history. (*dream/nightmare; problem/solution; freedom/slaves; cherished/spoiled; conserved/destroyed*) Then ask students to write a sentence explaining the author's idea that America is a paradox.

LINKING DISCIPLINES

History/African Studies

Have students look at the picture on page 140 and discuss the many aspects of African culture enslaved people brought with them to this country. Ask students to research foods (such as yams, peanuts, and okra), language (such as the words yam and goobers), musical instruments, and other African influences on American culture. Have them share their findings with the class.

---

1 Class Period   Homework: Student Study Guide p. 37

Chapter Summary

There is no greater paradox in American history than the presence of slavery in a nation founded on freedom. As the cotton empire expanded, the value of enslaved people climbed, their numbers doubled, and the slave system became more firmly entrenched in American society.

Key Vocabulary

hypocrisy   bigotry

1. CONNECT

Ask students to summarize what they already know about slavery in America or other countries.

2. UNDERSTAND

1. Read pages 138-140 up to "But a few people...." Explain: Slavery existed around the world for thousands of years. Ask: Why does the author call it a paradox in the United States? (*Slavery contradicted the ideal of freedom on which the nation was founded.*)
2. Read the rest of the chapter. Discuss: What was the colonization movement, and who supported it? (*It was a movement to send African-Americans to Africa, which was supported by Jefferson, Clay, and others who thought that blacks and whites could not live together; it was also supported by a few blacks.*)

3. CHECK UNDERSTANDING

Writing   Have students write a paragraph that explains why the institution of slavery was a paradox in the young republic.

Thinking About the Chapter (Drawing Conclusions)   Engage the class in a discussion of the factors that led to a large population of enslaved people, even when an 1808 law banished the slave trade. (*Students should mention that the slave trade was so profitable that people continued to buy and sell slaves even after importing Africans was declared illegal.*)

CHAPTER 28 | A MAN WHO DIDN'T DO AS HIS NEIGHBORS DID
PAGES 142-145

1 Class Period   Homework: Student Study Guide p. 38

Chapter Summary
Robert Carter III, a wealthy plantation owner from Virginia, and Henry Laurens, a rich South Carolina planter and slave trader, were unlikely people to wrestle with the moral issues of slavery, but they did.

Key Vocabulary
established church   dissenting church
emancipated   Age of Reason

1. CONNECT

Ask students to describe what they know about people who dare to be different. What virtues or moral courage might it take to do something that you believe is right when it is different from what everybody else does?

2. UNDERSTAND

1. Read pages 142-144 up to "But it was what Robert Carter did in 1791...." Discuss: In what ways was Robert Carter III unusual? *(He was born into a rich family, but wasn't interested in wealth. He was a religious man who changed his religion, and was concerned about freedom of religion and the meaning of life.)*
2. Read the rest of the chapter. Discuss: In what ways were Robert Carter III and Henry Laurens alike? *(Both were rich and owned slaves, but felt that slavery was morally wrong, so they freed the African-Americans on their plantations.)*

3. CHECK UNDERSTANDING

Writing   Ask students to write a one-paragraph biography of Robert Carter III that describes his family and lifestyle as well as his exemplary actions.

Thinking About the Chapter (Analyzing)   Engage the class in a discussion about King Carter and his grandson Robert Carter III. Ask students to describe the character of each and to infer what the legacy of each was. *(King Carter was a ruthless and greedy land grabber and his legacy was probably hardship for many. Robert Carter III was a man more interested in the meaning of life than money and his legacy was freedom for many.)*

MORE ABOUT...

Athens

Once (ca. 400 B.C.) the dominant city-state in Greece, Athens was for hundreds of years the center of government, arts, philosophy, and science in the ancient world. Leaders such as Pericles (government), Euripides (drama), Aristotle and Plato (philosophy), and Euclid (mathematics) lived there, and the beauty of its ancient ruins attest to the great structures the Greeks built. Places where brilliant leaders, wealth, and magnificent structures come together are often compared to Athens, as the Northern Neck of Virginia was.

READING NONFICTION

Analyzing Primary and Secondary Sources

Ask students to write a one-paragraph personal response to the primary sources on pages 146 and 147. Have volunteers read their paragraphs. Then discuss the author included these primary sources. (*Students should realize that the author included these first-hand accounts to show just how cruel and inhumane slavery was.*)

LINKING DISCIPLINES

History/Social Relations

Although slavery is a difficult subject to face, it is necessary to address it when learning about our country. The following words about slavery from a student named Ravi were cited in *Social Education*, Vol. 62, No. 6: "They need to deal with it. That's like the question of race today. It's like people saying, 'I don't want to talk about it.' I mean, other countries have to deal with genocide or the Holocaust. If you say you don't want to deal with it because it's a touchy issue, that's the exact reason why you have to do it. Otherwise, how can you move on if you say, 'We're just going to try to forget about slavery.'"

CHAPTER 29 AFRICAN-AMERICANS

PAGES 146–149

1 Class Period **Homework: Student Study Guide p. 39**

Chapter Summary

Many enslaved people, free blacks, and whites spoke out against slavery.

Key Vocabulary

oppressions pastor auction

1. CONNECT

Ask students to describe what they already know about the experience of African-Americans, both enslaved and free, in the early republic.

2. UNDERSTAND

1. Read pages 146-147 up to "James Forten served. . . ." Discuss: How did blacks win the right to vote in Massachusetts? *(Paul Cuffe refused to pay taxes without being able to vote. He lost, but Massachusetts passed a law giving blacks the same rights as whites.)*
2. Read the rest of the chapter. Discuss: How would you describe the institution of slavery? What basic human rights were denied? *(Students should describe slavery as an inhumane system that violated basic human rights. They should note that people were bought and sold, families were broken up, and slaves were denied the most basic freedoms.)*

3. CHECK UNDERSTANDING

Writing Ask students to write entries on Paul Cuffe and Richard Allen for a biographical dictionary.

Thinking About the Chapter (Summarizing/Drawing Conclusions) Have students review the chapter and summarize the oppressions of enslaved Africans using general categories. *(for example, beatings, being sold, having families broken up, being forced to do labor, being considered property)* Have students conclude what effects all of these actions had on slaves and slave owners.

HISTORY ARCHIVES

A History of US Sourcebook

#36, From *A North Carolina Law Forbidding the Teaching of Slaves to Read and Write* (1831)

1 Class Period   Homework: Student Study Guide p. 40

Chapter Summary

The cotton gin turned slavery into the foundation of a new empire that reached from the Atlantic across the South into Texas.

Key Vocabulary

coffle   lynch   yeoman farmers

1. CONNECT

Ask students to describe what they already know about the relationship between cotton and slavery. To refresh their memories, have a volunteer read the fourth and fifth paragraphs on page 107.

2. UNDERSTAND

1. Read page 150. Discuss: The invention of the cotton gin gave birth to a new South. How far did the new South extend? *(The new South stretched from the frontier of the former Southern Colonies through Mississippi and Louisiana, and all the way to Texas.)*
2. Read the rest of the chapter. Ask: How did white Southerners' attitudes toward slavery change after cotton became king? *(from believing that slavery was wrong but not knowing how to end it to believing that slavery was good and necessary)*
3. Graph: Have students use Resource Page 9 (TG 115) to create line graphs and answer questions about cotton production and the enslaved population.

3. CHECK UNDERSTANDING

Writing   Ask students to pretend that they are Thomas Jefferson visiting the New South in a time machine. Have them write a paragraph from Jefferson's point of view describing changes in slavery and his reactions.

Thinking About the Chapter (Comparing and Contrasting)
Have the class compare the South in Washington's and Jefferson's time with the South in Andrew Jackson's time. How did its size, ideas, and leaders change? *(The New South was larger, stretching all the way to Texas; slavery became more cruel and widespread and ideas supporting slavery, more common; the new leaders in the South no longer came from rich, well-educated families, and many were more ruthless than their predecessors.)*

JOHNS HOPKINS TEAM LEARNING

OPINIONS ABOUT EXPANSIONISM

1 CLASS PERIOD

JOHNS HOPKINS
U N I V E R S I T Y

FOCUS ACTIVITY

1. Divide the class into teams of four students each. Ask each team to discuss wh[...] pens in a country or region when there is a deeply rooted conflict—either between two distinct groups or two clashing points of view. (*Students may say that such conflicts often lead to violence and social change.*)

2. Ask teams to **Brainstorm** places in the world in which such conflicts exist today, for instance, in the Middle East (between Israelis and Palestinians).

3. Have teams discuss how power, identity, and growth affect deeply rooted conflicts. (*If one side is more powerful, it may suppress the opposition.*)

STUDENT TEAM LEARNING ACTIVITY/ANALYZING TWO SIDES OF THE COIN

1. Have teams use **Think-Team-Share** to respond to this question: How might settlers and Native Americans have solved their conflicts and lived successfully together? (*Students may suggest that the two groups could have come up with an equitable way to share the land.*)

2. To have students explore both sides of this issue, or two sides of the coin, have teams divide into partnerships. Give each partner one of the following opinion cards:

Opinion 1: We were here first. No one can own the land. The settlers should not have taken what did not belong to them.
Opinion 2: The Indians should have become like us. They stood in the way of change and progress. If they had changed, they would have survived.

3. Give partners five minutes to jot down as many reasons or details as possible supporting their assigned opinions.

4. Sharing Information Each partner gets one minute to state and support his or her position to the other partner. The two partners then work together to try to find some middle ground on which they can compromise so that they can live together. (They may find that they cannot reach an acceptable compromise.)

5. Circulate and Monitor As the partnerships work, systematically visit them and help students read, locate, and record appropriate information.

6. When partnerships are finished, have each team come together to evaluate their work.

7. With the class, discuss the "two sides of the coin" and whether peaceful coexistence was possible at that time for settlers and Native Americans. Elicit that even if the government wanted to, it could not stop westward expansion. Have students analyze the ethics of the settlers' behavior.

ASSESSMENT

Part 6 Check-Up   Use Check-Up 6 (TG page 105) to assess student learning in Part 6.

ALTERNATE ASSESSMENT
Ask students to write an essay answering the following question, which links the big ideas across chapters:

Making Connections   How did the invention of the cotton gin contribute to the oppression of both southern Indians and blacks? *(It caused the cotton empire to expand. This in turn led to the removal of southern Indians from agricultural land. The demand for and value of slaves went up, ending any possibility of a peaceful end to slavery.)*

DEBATING THE ISSUES
Use the topic below to stimulate debate.

Resolved   "…if the law is of such a nature that it requires you to be an agent of injustice to another, then I say, break the law.…" (Henry David Thoreau, 1849) Have students consider this statement as they take various sides on the issue of Indian removal: Cherokees, Seminoles, homesteaders, soldiers (see Colonel Hitchcock's statement on page 136 of the Student Edition), Andrew Jackson, and John Marshall.

MAKING ETHICAL JUDGMENTS
The following activity asks students to consider issues of ethics.

Suppose that you were a soldier assigned to force the Cherokee people from their homes into stockades, and then force them on a march thousands of miles to the West. Would you refuse? Remember that doing so would be against the law and you would face a court martial. Would you agree? Would you make the best of the situation?

To help the discussion, read the following passage written by a soldier more than 50 years after the ordeal (John G. Burnett, McClellan's Company, Second Regiment, Second Brigade, Mounted Infantry, Part of the 1838-1839 Removal):

> *Future generations will read and condemn the act and I do hope posterity will remember that private soldiers like myself…had no choice in the matter.…However murder is murder whether committed by the villain skulking in the dark or by uniformed men stepping to the strains of martial music.*
>
> *Murder is murder and somebody must answer, somebody must explain…the four-thousand silent graves that mark the trail.…I wish I could forget it all, but the picture of six-hundred and forty-five wagons lumbering over the frozen ground with their Cargo of suffering humanity still lingers in my memory.*

USING THE RUBRICS

To assess these writing assignments, group projects, and activities, scoring rubrics have been provided at the back to this Teaching Guide. Be sure to explain the rubrics to your students.

Researching Systems for Writing   Have the class work in groups, choosing systems of writing to research and report on. If any students are familiar with other alphabets, they should demonstrate how they are used.

Reenacting History   Have students work in groups to reenact a scene of their choosing from Part 6. Some possibilities are: (a) Robert Carter III tells his family that he is going to free the family's slaves. The family responds. (b) Men and women of the Seminole nation decide whether to move west of the Mississippi or to go to war with the United States. (c) A white woman in Virginia is arrested for teaching free blacks how to read.

Writing Letters Home   Imagine you are a private in the U.S. Army, fighting the Seminole in the swamps of Florida. Write a letter home describing one day from beginning to end.

Writing Newspaper Articles   Imagine you are Elizabeth Freeman. Write an article for publication in the Vox Africanorum column in the *Maryland Gazette*. Describe your case and give some helpful advice for other blacks.

Designing Posters   On January 1, 2008, the nation will celebrate the 200th anniversary of the act of Congress outlawing the slave trade. Design a poster commemorating the event.

Linking Past and Present   In 1900 the first sewing machines arrived in southern Florida. With them the Seminole women developed a unique way of sewing patterns. Today Seminole clothing is known around the world for its beautiful and intricate designs. In the library media center, students can find some examples and copy them for display.

LOOKING AHEAD

Analyzing an Advertisement

Read the following advertisement from newspapers of the period.

> *$50 Reward.—Ran away from the subscriber, his negro man Pauladore, commonly called Paul. I understand Gen. R. Y. Hayne has purchased his wife and children from H. L. Pinckney, Esq. and has them now on his plantation at Goosecreek, where, no doubt, the fellow is frequently lurking.*

Ask students for their reactions. How does hearing this ad make them feel? Explain that as the slave population grew, it became more difficult for slave owners to continue to enslave people. More such ads were run. More people saw them and began to feel that slavery was wrong. The issue divided the nation. In Part 7 students will hear the voices from both sides of what was to become a great debate.

THE BIG IDEAS

In 1848, the usual debates characteristic of the American electoral process reached the boiling point. Jefferson Davis accused Northerners of using the issue of slavery for their own gain. He charged:

> *What do you propose?…Do you propose to better the condition of the slave? Not at all.…You desire to weaken the political power of the southern states; and why? Because you want, by an unjust system of legislation, to promote the industry of the New England states, at the expense of the people of the South and their industry.*

The regionalism of the past gave way to sectionalism as industry developed the North and cotton cultivation determined the Southern economy. Both societies sought to control the laws of the land. In the conflict, each section looked to the West to tip the balance in its favor.

INTRODUCING PART 7

SETTING GOALS

Introduce Part 7 by writing its title, "Debating the Issues," on the chalkboard. Ask students to identify the issues—large and small—that were pulling sections of the nation in opposite directions. (*Students should identify the greatest issues of the day—states' rights and slavery—and other issues, such as tariffs and the development of the West.*)

To set goals for Part 7, tell students that they will
- describe the roles and importance of William Lloyd Garrison, Frederick Douglass, Henry Clay, John Calhoun, Daniel Webster, and Robert Young Hayne.
- debate the ethical implications when elected officials follow their conscience instead of representing the views of their constituents.
- analyze how geography—specifically rivers—influenced the settlement and expansion of the nation in the 1800s.

SETTING A CONTEXT FOR READING

Thinking About the Big Ideas   The debates and issues of the 19th century came out of real differences between the North, the South, and the West. Read the passages below, taken from three diaries, and have students identify each region and analyze the lifestyle each entry portrayed:

(a) *Up before day, at the clang of a bell,—and out of the mill by the clang of the bell—into the mill, and at work in obedience to that ding-dong of a bell—just as though we were so many living machines.* (Northern mill worker)

(b) *The fastest hoer takes the lead row. He is usually about a rod in advance of his companions. If one of them passes him, he is whipped. If one falls behind or is a moment idle, he is whipped.* (Southern slave describing cultivating cotton)

(c) Traveled 14 miles over the worst road that was ever made, up and down, very steep, rough and rocky hills, through mud holes, twisting and winding round stumps, logs and fallen trees....We hear the road is still worse ahead. (woman on a Western trail)

Ask: What kind of life does each person describe? How can you tell where each quote is from? What does this tell you? What happens when the daily problems found in one place are so different from the problems found in another? *(Lead the students to understand that in the early 19th century, regional differences grew so fast and were so great that common bonds were shrinking.)*

Identifying Cause and Effect   The issue of slavery increasingly divided the North and South. As students read about the polarizing effects of the issue, have them keep in mind the causes and effects of the regional differences. *(The South was an agricultural society based on plantation crops such as cotton, rice, and tobacco, which required large amounts of labor, which encouraged slavery. The North had many developing industrial centers and ports. Immigrants flocked to the North to work in the factories there.)*

SETTING A CONTEXT IN SPACE AND TIME
Visualizing Regions   The great debates of the time—over slavery, tariffs, states' rights, Western transportation—were all rooted in places. Each issue could be linked with a region; for example, slavery with the South. To help students better understand these different regions, have them turn to the feature on pages 160-161. Ask volunteers to each read aloud a paragraph or so as you or other students locate the places on a large map of the United States.

Understanding Change over Time   The period covered in Part 7 overlaps events described earlier. Have students record on the class time line key events (such as the Missouri Compromise) and events in the lives of key people (such as Frederick Douglass). This will help students keep track of simultaneous events and trends. For example the Trail of Tears began in 1838, a few years before Frederick Douglass spoke on Nantucket.

31 ABOLITIONISTS WANT TO END SLAVERY

CHAPTER

PAGES 153–156

1 Class Period   **Homework: Student Study Guide p. 41**

Chapter Summary

The argument for and against slavery heats up the existing regional differences between the North and South.

Key Vocabulary

abolition   Missouri Compromise   secede

1. CONNECT

Ask students to describe what they already know about the people who hated slavery and wanted to end it. Have a volunteer read the paragraph beginning "But a few people..." on page 140.

2. UNDERSTAND

1. Read page 153. Discuss: What did Jefferson mean when he wrote, "We have the wolf by the ears, and we can neither hold him nor safely let him go"? *(Slavery was like a dangerous wild animal that could not be controlled but whose release would threaten its captors.)*
2. Read the rest of the chapter. Discuss: How did the Missouri Compromise keep the peace between North and South? *(By admitting Maine as a free state and Missouri as a slave state, the compromise maintained the balance of power in Congress.)*

3. CHECK UNDERSTANDING

Writing Have students write a paragraph explaining the factors that caused the North and South to take opposing sides on slavery.

Thinking About the Chapter (Identifying Problem and Solution) Engage the class in a discussion of the problem caused when Missouri wanted to enter the union as a slave state. *(Students should note that if Missouri entered as a slave state, there would be 13 slave states and 12 free states, tipping the balance in Congress to pro-slavery states.)* Ask students to describe the solution to this problem. *(The solution was the Missouri Compromise, whereby Missouri was admitted as a slave state, Maine as a free state, and it was agreed that no future slave state would be admitted above 36°30'.)*

ACTIVITIES/JOHNS HOPKINS TEAM LEARNING

See the Student Team Learning Activity on TG page 95.

MORE ABOUT...

Denmark Vesey

A free man and a carpenter in Charleston, South Carolina, Denmark Vesey said that he was very satisfied with his own condition, but having once been enslaved, he was determined to free his people. Vesey planned and organized what could have become the largest slave revolt in the country, had he not been betrayed in the end.

Small Group Activity

Distribute Resource Page 11 (Teaching Guide p. 117) to the class and have them read "Reflections, Occasioned by the late Disturbances in Charleston." Have student break into groups to discuss the questions following the passage.

LINKING DISCIPLINES

Geography/Math

Have students use a map to trace the water route of a barrel of goods from Cincinnati to New York City and estimate the total distance traveled. (One route would be to take the Ohio River to the Mississippi and then to the Gulf of Mexico, around Florida, and north to New York.)

HISTORY ARCHIVES

A History of US Sourcebook

1. #36, From *A North Carolina Law Forbidding the Teaching of Slaves to Read and Write* (1831)

2. #47, From Frederick Douglass, *Fourth of July Oration* (1852)

1 Class Period   **Homework: Student Study Guide p. 42**

Chapter Summary

Frederick Douglass bravely spoke of his own experiences as a slave and worked for human rights for all oppressed people.

Key Vocabulary

freeman   slave catchers

1. CONNECT

Ask students to discuss several African-Americans in the past century who have struggled to ensure justice and equality for all people. *(Students' should identify Martin Luther King, Jr., and Malcolm X.)* Then ask the class to describe nineteenth-century African-Americans who performed a similar role. *(Frederick Douglass, Harriet Tubman, Sojourner Truth, and others)*

2. UNDERSTAND

1. Read pages 157-159. Ask: What did Frederick Douglass mean when he said, "Justice to the Negro is safety to the nation"? How could slavery endanger a democracy? *(Students should note that as long as there was the injustice of slavery, the nation risked being torn apart by violent struggles, and democracy might not survive.)*

2. Read pages 160-161. Discuss: What role did rivers play in the settlement and expansion of the nation? *(Rivers such as the Ohio and Mississippi were superhighways transporting people and their possessions in addition to manufactured goods. River travel was faster than overland travel, allowing more people to be moved west more rapidly. This led to the expansion of the nation.)*

3. CHECK UNDERSTANDING

Writing   Ask students to write a one-paragraph biography of Frederick Douglass and his achievements.

Thinking About the Chapter (Making Inferences)   Have the class discuss how Douglass dealt with the limits imposed on him by slavery. *(using his wits to learn how to read and write, keeping the hope of freedom to keep from killing himself)* Discuss why a person who has been oppressed, like Douglass, would want to help others, even though they may be oppressed for different reasons.

33 NAMING PRESIDENTS

PAGES 162–168

1 Class Period   Homework: Student Study Guide p. 43

Chapter Summary

The eight presidents who followed Andrew Jackson are not as well remembered as the first seven. None held office for more than one term.

Key Vocabulary

Free Soilers

1. CONNECT

Ask students to name the first seven presidents in order. (*George Washington, John Adams, Thomas Jefferson, James Madison, James Monroe, John Quincy Adams, Andrew Jackson*)

2. UNDERSTAND

1. Read pages 162-165. Ask students to use these clues to name the presidents: the hardest working man in the country (*Polk*); Old Tippecanoe (*Harrison*); Old Kinderhook (*Van Buren*).
2. Read the rest of the chapter. Have students name these presidents: "An old fool," Andrew Jackson said of him: "I would have sent him to the North Pole if we had kept a minister there!" (*Buchanan*); Old Rough and Ready (*Taylor*); His Accidency (*Tyler*).

3. CHECK UNDERSTANDING

Writing Ask students to write an imaginary dialogue between the third and fifteenth presidents. The dialogue should include what the two men would say to each other about slavery.

Thinking About the Chapter (Synthesizing) Have students review the maps and text on pages 163-165. Then ask them to describe the extent of the nation and identify the new states that were added to the country in the 1830s (*Michigan, Arkansas*), and name the presidents during that decade. (*Jackson, Van Buren*). Repeat for the 1840s (*Texas, Iowa, Wisconsin: Harrison, Tyler, Polk, Taylor*) and the 1850s. (*California, Minnesota, Oregon, Kansas; Fillmore, Pierce, Buchanan.*)

READING NONFICTION

Analyzing Graphic Aids

Have students tell what the color red signifies on the maps on pages 162-164. (*Red indicates a state that became part of the United States during the decade in the map's title.*) Ask: What does the dark tan color mean? (*land that was a U.S. territory during the decade in the map's title*) Have students explain how they know this. (*The information can be inferred from the captions on each page.*)

GEOGRAPHY CONNECTIONS

Using the maps on pages 162-164, have students determine in which decade the United States added the most territory. (*1840-1850*) Which territories and states were added then? (*the West and Southwest*) Have students draw conclusions about why it took four decades for the nation to acquire the territory to the west of the Louisiana Purchase lands. (*Possible responses: The nation had to settle the huge Louisiana territory first; the U.S. saw little value in the western lands.*)

MORE ABOUT...

Capitol Hygiene

Read aloud the following quote from British writer Charles Dickens about his visit to the Capitol during Tyler's presidency. Ask students to pay attention to the writer's humorous tone. "Both Houses are handsomely carpeted; but the state to which these carpets are reduced by the universal disregard of the spittoon...and the extraordinary improvements on the pattern which are squirted and dabbled upon it in every direction, do not admit of being described....I strongly recommend all strangers not to look at the floor; and if they happen to drop anything,...not to pick it up with an ungloved hand on any account."

READING NONFICTION

Analyzing Point of View

Point out to students that Joy Hakim often expresses her opinions loudly and clearly. Have students cite examples of her opinions of Clay, Calhoun, and Webster. Then ask how she expresses her opinion in the sidebar about Daniel Webster on page 171. (*She says Daniel, You're Wrong! in the title.*)

MEETING INDIVIDUAL NEEDS

Have volunteers prepare and perform a debate between Clay and Webster on the value of the West. The student role playing Webster can use the Daniel, You're Wrong! feature on page 171.

HISTORY ARCHIVES

A History of US Sourcebook

#37, From Andrew Jackson, *Proclamation to the People of South Carolina* (1832)

34 | A TRIUMVIRATE IS THREE PEOPLE

CHAPTER

PAGES 169–172

1 Class Period   Homework: Student Study Guide p. 44

Chapter Summary
As the conflict over slavery drove a wedge between the nation's sections, three great orators held sway in Congress. One spoke for a divided West, one for the North, and one for the South.

Key Vocabulary
triumvirate   tariff
oratory   Whig

1. CONNECT

Ask students to describe what they have learned in previous chapters about Henry Clay, Daniel Webster, and John Calhoun. (Refer students to the third paragraph on page 129 and to page 150, the paragraph beginning "Most of the newly rich men....")

2. UNDERSTAND

1. Read pages 169-170. Discuss: Each of the three great orators—Henry Clay, Daniel Webster, and John C. Calhoun—represented the interests of a different region. Which region did each man speak for? (*Webster spoke for the North; Clay, the West; and Calhoun, the South.*)
2. Read the rest of the chapter. Discuss: What did Webster think about developing the West? Do you think Clay would agree or disagree? (*Webster thought the West to be worthless. Clay would disagree, because he represented that region.*)

3. CHECK UNDERSTANDING

Writing   Ask students to imagine they are directing a play about Clay, Webster, and Calhoun. Have students write a character profile of each man for the actors.

Thinking About the Chapter (Drawing Conclusions)   All three of these men wanted to be president, but none of them came close. Have students draw conclusions about why these men were unsuccessful in their national ambitions. They should present evidence from the chapter to support their conclusions. (*Possible response: Each was so closely identified with the interests of one section that he couldn't get enough votes nationwide to win.*)

35 THE GREAT DEBATE

PAGES 173–176

1 Class Period   Homework: Student Study Guide p. 45

Chapter Summary

The future of slavery rested on this question: Which was supreme—federal law or state law? The debate between the North and South raged as both sides looked to the West to tip the balance of power.

Key Vocabulary

secession   sovereign

1. CONNECT

Ask students if they are citizens of your state or of the United States. Elicit that we all have dual citizenry—state and national. Explain that in 1830, many Americans thought of themselves as citizens of their states, not of the United States.

2. UNDERSTAND

1. Read pages 173-174 up to "Picture a big man...." Discuss: Who is debating in Congress, and what is each man's position? *(Robert Young Hayne is trying to get the West to support states' rights and oppose tariffs; Daniel Webster is arguing for a strong Union and against any move toward disunion on the part of the South.)*
2. Read the rest of the chapter. Discuss: Why is it important for Hayne and Webster to win the support of the Western senators? *(Without their support, neither North nor South can get what they want.)*

3. CHECK UNDERSTANDING

Writing   Have students imagine that they are in the Senate gallery for the great debate. Have them write a brief letter to a friend in the West describing the event.

Thinking About the Chapter (Making Inferences)   Challenge students to explain how the issues of states' rights and slavery were linked. *(Students should realize that if states held the supreme power, the future of slavery in the South would be secure. If the federal government had supreme power, slavery could be declared illegal.)*

READING NONFICTION

Analyzing Rhetorical Devices

You may want to get a copy of Webster's speech for students to read. One source is www.dartmouth.edu/~dwebster/. Distribute parts of the speech to small groups of students, and have them circle rhetorical devices such as repetition, figurative language, imagery, loaded words, and so on. Have the class come together to analyze the devices that Webster uses.

1 Class Period   Homework: Student Study Guide p. 46

Chapter Summary

Book Four concludes with a note of encouragement and a promise that great progress would be made toward the splendid goal set by the Founding Fathers.

1. CONNECT

Ask students to discuss how democracy has evolved in America up to this point. Ask: Which groups of people are enjoying the benefits of democracy? Why hasn't justice, freedom, and equality been extended to all citizens?

2. UNDERSTAND

1. Read page 177. Discuss: What do Andrew Jackson's last words tell us about the dominant concerns and feelings of this period? *(His words reveal that concerns about race and slavery ran very deep.)*
2. What major issues are "testing" the nation in the mid-1800s? *(The major issues are slavery and conflicts between whites and Native Americans.)*

3. CHECK UNDERSTANDING

Writing   Ask students to write a paragraph answering the author's question: "How do you think the nation is doing?"

Thinking About the Chapter (Making Predictions)   Ask students to predict what will happen to the nation. Have the class brainstorm answers to questions such as the following: Will regional differences undermine the nation's unity? How will the issue of slavery be resolved? What will happen to Native Americans? *(Students may say that differences between the South and North will divide the nation, the Civil War will be fought to keep the nation united and to end slavery, and conflict between Native Americans and settlers will increase.)*

JOHNS HOPKINS TEAM LEARNING

FREE STATES VERSUS SLAVE STATES

1 EXTENDED CLASS PERIOD

FOCUS ACTIVITY

1. Have students work in partnerships, with one student in each pair taking the part of an abolitionist or a planter.

2. Ask partnerships to role play how they feel about slavery.

STUDENT TEAM LEARNING ACTIVITY/MAPPING THE MISSOURI COMPROMISE

1. Combine partnerships into teams of four students. Have teams use **Round Robin** to **Brainstorm** the feelings of abolitionists and southern planters on the issue of slavery. Then have each team create two word webs: one for abolitionists and one for planters.

2. Have teams divide into partnerships again. Distribute a copy of Resource Page 5 (TG page 111) and three different-colored markers, crayons, or pencils to each pair. Tell students to reread Chapter 31 to identify free states, slave states, and latitude 36°30'.

3. Have partners choose colors to represent free states and slave states in 1820, color them in on the map, and make a map key. Next, they should draw in the 36°30' parallel across the lands of the Louisiana Territory. (Tell students that the line corresponds to the long southern border of Missouri.) Finally, have them color Missouri and Maine with the appropriate colors.

4. Sharing Information Have each partnership rejoin its team and share its map. Team members may want to double-check one another's maps.

5. Circulate and Monitor As students work, systematically visit them. If necessary, help students locate states. Explain that in 1820, West Virginia was still part of Virginia and not a separate state. If necessary, help students create the map key.

6. Ask teams to discuss the following questions:
* What would you think of the terms of the Missouri Compromise if you were a Southerner? A Northerner?
* Do you think that the Missouri Compromise could be a lasting solution to the issue of slavery? Why or why not?
* What solution would you have suggested?

SUMMARIZING PART 7

USING THE RUBRICS
To assess these writing assignments, group projects, and activities, scoring rubrics have been provided at the back to this Teaching Guide. Be sure to explain the rubrics to your students.

ASSESSMENT

Part 7 Check-Up   Use Check-Up 7 (TG page 106) to assess student learning in Part 7.

ALTERNATE ASSESSMENT
Ask students to write an essay answering one of the following questions, which link the big ideas across chapters:

1. Making Connections   Why might Southerners fear the power of a Northern-controlled Congress? (*Northern interests contradicted their own, especially on tariffs and slavery.*)

2. Making Connections   Why might abolitionists argue against states' rights? (*Abolitionists hoped to end slavery in all states. If states' rights were accepted, slavery would persist in the Southern states.*)

DEBATING THE ISSUES
Use the topic below to stimulate debate.

Resolved   That the ultimate authority rests in the states, and that they have the right to nullify a federal law that they do not agree with. (Have students argue the issue of states' rights by assigning one group to represent Hayne and Calhoun, another to argue for Daniel Webster, and a third to represent Andrew Jackson.)

MAKING ETHICAL JUDGMENTS
The following activity asks students to consider issues of ethics.

Sam Houston hated slavery and boldly spoke out against it. But Sam Houston was a senator. The people of Texas sent him to represent their interests in Congress, and Texas was pro-slavery. Should Sam Houston have spoken in the Senate in favor of slavery? (To encourage discussion, have students suppose the reverse case: What if a senator from Massachusetts happened to be for slavery?)

PROJECTS AND ACTIVITIES
Using Mnemonics   Students can make up their own mnemonic devices to remember the names of the first 15 presidents. They should try to take words from a topic that interests them, such as sports or music.

Writing a Pamphlet   Ask students to finish this pamphlet started by Theodore Weld, the most widely read abolitionist writer.

> *Reader, you are impaneled as a juror to try a plain case and bring in an honest verdict. The question at issue is not one of law but of fact—What is the actual condition of the slaves of the United States? A plainer case never went to a jury. Look at it. Twenty-seven hundred thousand persons in this country, men, women, and children, are in slavery....*

Writing Campaign Slogans   In the early 19th century, every candidate had at least one nickname, and these were sometimes used in campaign slogans. For example, one slogan used in Zachary Taylor's campaign was "Old Rough and Ready never surrenders." Have students choose three presidents and write campaign slogans for them.

Writing a Biography   Frederick Douglass changed his life dramatically. He began his life in enslavement but ended up as a famous abolitionist and presidential adviser. How did he do it? Have students research and report on the life of this fascinating American.

Speaking Out   Have students review Daniel Webster's assertion that the West was a vast, worthless wasteland. Then, ask teams of students to prepare a short oral statement in which a senator from a new Western state defends his region.

Reenacting History   Divide the class into eight groups to design short skits based on the eight presidents from Van Buren to Buchanan. Tell students the challenge is to portray their character without ever mentioning his name. After each skit is performed, the rest of the class should try to identify the president.

LOOKING AHEAD

Predicting the Future

In 1864, Abraham Lincoln wrote:

> The world has never had a good definition of the word liberty. And the American people just now are much in want of one. We all declare for liberty; but in using the same word we do not mean the same thing. With some, the word liberty may mean for each man to do as he pleases with himself and the product of his labor; while with others the same word may mean for some men to do as they please with other men and the product of other men's labor. Here are two, not only different, but incompatible things, called by the same name, liberty.

Ask: Which two groups is Lincoln talking about? (*Those for and against slavery*) What groups had conflicting ideas of liberty in the West? In the North? (*settlers and Native Americans, factory workers and factory owners*)

Explain that in the next period, the power of northern industry would continue to grow, the frontier would move farther west, and cotton would reign in the South. Ask students to speculate about what conflicts the nation will face in the coming years.

SYNTHESIZING THE BIG IDEAS IN BOOK FOUR

Use the following questions to help students pull together some of the major concepts and themes covered in this book. Note: You may wish to assign these as essay questions for assessment.

1. Describe the major differences between the Federalists and Democratic-Republicans as represented by Hamilton and Jefferson. Issues to consider include: who should have power to govern; strong federal government versus states' rights; the importance of agriculture and business. *(Hamilton had faith in the educated aristocracy, believed in a strong federal government, and felt that the government should create a positive environment for business. Jefferson believed in democracy, with the common man empowered; he believed in states' rights and feared a central government that grew too strong; he did not believe that the government should aid business and thought the foundation of democracy was in farming.)*

2. As settlers pushed west and south into Indian lands, the Native Americans attempted to adapt, to resist, or to band together and stop the invasion. Describe how Tecumseh, Osceola, and Sequoyah illustrate these strategies for survival. *(Tecumseh attempted to unify the tribes in order to stop the invasion. Osceola led the Seminole people in a war of resistance. Sequoyah, by developing an alphabet for the Cherokee language, helped his people to adapt to the ways of white Americans. Very quickly, most Cherokee people became literate.)*

3. John Adams said: "My gift of John Marshall to the people of the United States was the proudest act of my life." What did we the people gain by that appointment? *(John Marshall helped rebalance the branches of the government by giving the judicial branch the power to determine the constitutionality of a law through judicial review.)*

4. In the early part of the nineteenth century, a uniquely American foreign policy was developed. George Washington believed that the new nation should not involve itself with other nation's affairs—and vice versa. Did other presidents agree with Washington? *(For the most part, they did. Under John Adams, the Alien and Sedition acts were aimed at protecting the nation from foreign influences. Although Madison resisted, War Hawks urged the United States into the War of 1812. Things changed under Monroe, however. Monroe perfected Washington's policy in the Monroe Doctrine when he declared Americans hostile to European meddling in the Western Hemisphere.)*

5. How did the Industrial Revolution cause the North and the South to develop differently? *(The North had the waterpower needed to drive machines, so industry developed rapidly there, causing the region to become urban and industrial. The cotton gin made it profitable to grow cotton across the South, causing the South to remain rural and dependent on slavery.)*

6. As the Constitution was ratified, there were those present who saw the seeds of future conflict around the issue of slavery. What events in the first half of the nineteenth century can be found to support those fears? *(Students should cite the slave revolts, the growing abolitionist movement, and the violence that surrounded the issue.)*

7. What was the basis of the great debate between Robert Young Hayne, representing Southern interests, and Daniel Webster, representing the North? *(Hayne was looking to the Western states for support, to knock down a tariff by supporting the right of states to strike down federal laws. Daniel Webster won Western support for the federal government.)*

8. Read aloud the following quote from Thomas Jefferson.

Men by their constitutions are naturally divided into two parties: (1) Those who fear and mistrust the people, and wish to draw all powers from them into the hands of the higher classes, (2) Those who identify themselves with the people, have confidence in them, cherish and consider them as the most honest and safe, although not the most wise depository of the public interests.

Choose several of the leading figures you have read about in Book Four. Which view best describes the political views of each one? *(Responses will vary.)*

CHECK-UP 1

Answering the following questions will help you understand and remember what you have read in Chapters 1-5. Write your answers on a separate sheet of paper.

1. The people listed below played key roles in events described in Chapters 1–5. Describe the connections between the two people in each pair of names and tell what each one did that was important in this period of our history.
   a. Thomas Jefferson, Alexander Hamilton
   b. Benjamin Banneker, Charles L'Enfant
   c. George Washington, John Adams

2. America's rivers and mountains were important role in the new nation. Explain the importance of the following in 1790.
   a. Mississippi River
   b. Potomac River
   c. Appalachian Mountains

3. In the first administration, many terms were used to describe the factions and parties that developed. Define each term and name one person associated with it.
   a. Conservatives
   b. Liberals
   c. Federalists
   d. Republicans

4. The nation developed a capitalist society. Describe what that is, using the following terms.
   a. capital
   b. credit
   c. collateral
   d. default
   e. investors
   f. speculators
   g. free-enterprise system

5. The nation experienced a huge population explosion. Explain how each of the following contributed.
   a. cheap land
   b. healthy environment
   c. conditions in Europe

6. The debate for and against a strong government raged in those early years. Describe the argument each of the following would have made.
   a. someone who feared the masses
   b. someone who wanted to protect individual rights
   c. someone who wanted to encourage industry

7. Democracy was a threat to some and a hope to others. Describe how each of the following might have felt.
   a. European monarch
   b. European farmer with little land
   c. European farmer with a lot of land

8. **Thinking About the Big Ideas**   Explain why the year 1789 is a landmark in political history and how the events of that year continue to affect our lives.

Name _____   Date _____

CHECK-UP 2

Answering the following questions will help you understand and remember what you have read in Chapters 6-11. Write your answers on a separate sheet of paper.

1. Imagine a conversation between the two people in each pair below. Identify each person and write a few sentences that they might have said to each other.
   a. John Adams, Matthew Lyon
   b. Thomas Jefferson, John Marshall
   c. Alexander Hamilton, Aaron Burr
   d. William Clark, Meriwether Lewis
   e. Ca-me-ah-wait, Sacajawea

2. Write a description contrasting the borders of the United States before and after the Louisiana Purchase. These place names will help you.
   a. Mississippi River
   b. Missouri River
   c. Oregon Country
   d. New Orleans
   e. Mexico
   f. Rocky Mountains

3. Imagine that you are with the Lewis and Clark expedition. Write a newspaper article telling of your adventures from St. Louis to the Pacific Ocean. Use the following terms.
   a. portage
   b. river source
   c. river mouth
   d. Northwest Passage

4. Imagine you are Thomas Adams or Matthew Lyon. Write an opinion of the Alien and Sedition acts using these terms.
   a. abridge
   b. unconstitutional
   c. Bill of Rights

5. How did judicial review change our system of checks and balances?

6. How did Federalists and Democratic-Republicans differ on each of the following issues?
   a. strong central government
   b. war between France and England
   c. Alien and Sedition acts
   d. the French Revolution
   e. Virginia and Kentucky resolutions

7. Imagine that you could interview Thomas Jefferson. What would he say about the following?
   a. the common man
   b. human nature
   c. the purpose of government

8. Many different nations of Indians lived with in the area of the Louisiana Purchase. Imagine that you are a Plains Indian. Describe you hopes and fears now that you are part of the United States. (Remember that Indians, along with blacks and women, could not vote.)

9. **Thinking About the Big Ideas** As the beliefs of the Revolution and the Constitution were transformed into a working government, there were many disputes. But each faction adjusted. They came together to form an American way, a national character. Describe how you see the national character today and how it is related to the time period you have just studied.

CHECK-UP 3

Answering the following questions will help you understand and remember what you have read in Chapters 12-14. Write your answers on a separate sheet of paper.

1. Imagine a conversation between the two people in each pair below. Identify each person and write a few sentences that they might have said to each other.
   a. Red Jacket, Thomas Jefferson
   b. Tecumseh, Cherokee Chiefs
   c. the Prophet (Tenskwatawa), William Henry Harrison
   d. Osceola, Andrew Jackson

2. As new Americans pushed Native Americans west and south, the frontier moved farther into Indian lands. Describe the location of each of the following in relation to the moving frontier.
   a. the Iroquois in western New York
   b. the Shawnee in Ohio
   c. the Creek in Alabama

3. George Washington thought factions were destructive; Thomas Jefferson thought they were healthy. Describe how factionalism affected the Creek people.

4. It is 1805 and you are a reporter at a council between the Iroquois and missionaries. Write an article for your paper describing the event and the main points of Red Jacket's speech.

5. As more and more people pushed into Indian lands, Native Americans were forced to make hard choices. Explain who made each of the choices listed below and describe the circumstances. (Remember that many tribes made more than one choice.)
   a. fled to British Canada
   b. fled to Spanish Florida
   c. adapted to white ways
   d. lived with white neighbors but kept their old ways

6. Describe the views each of the following had of Native Americans.
   a. Thomas Jefferson
   b. Shakers
   c. William Henry Harrison

7. Conduct an imaginary interview with Tenskwatawa (the Prophet). Decide what questions you would most like to have asked him, and write the answers you think he would have made.

8. When Thomas Jefferson made the Louisiana Purchase, he thought that more eastern Indians such as the Iroquois, Cherokee, Shawnee, or Creek could move there. Write a letter to Thomas Jefferson explaining your opinion of his plan.

9. Explain the results of the Battles of Tippecanoe and Horseshoe Bend.

10. **Thinking About the Big Ideas**   On a separate sheet of paper, write a short paragraph about American Indians' efforts to survive. Use the words power, identity, and change in your answer.

CHECK-UP 4

Answering the following questions will help you understand and remember what you have read in Chapters 15-20. Write your answers on a separate sheet of paper.

1. Imagine a conversation between the two people in each pair below. Identify each person and write a few sentences that they might have said to each other.
   a. Captain Perry, Commodore Chauncey
   b. Major General Ross, Dolley Madison
   c. Mary Pickersgill, Francis Scott Key
   d. Osceola, Andrew Jackson
   e. Anne Royall, John Quincy Adams
   f. Thomas Jefferson, John Adams

2. Imagine you, like Elijah Fletcher, are traveling from region to region. Write your observations for each of the following.
   a. the North
   b. the South
   c. the West

3. How were the War Hawks of 1812 and the expansionists of the 1820s the same?

4. What were the main causes and results of the War of 1812?

5. In 1823 President Monroe said "…the American Continents…are henceforth not to be considered as subjects for future colonization by any European power." Describe possible reactions in each of the following.
   a. Europe
   b. The United States
   c. Latin America

6. Conduct an imaginary interview with the black soldiers sent to Captain Oliver Perry. Decide what questions you would most like to have asked them and write the responses you think they would have made.

7. Identify the speaker or writer of each of the following quotes.
   a. "Let the people rule."
   b. "Thomas Jefferson survives."
   c. "May the Lord bless King George, convert him, and take him to heaven, as we want no more of him."
   d. "Oh! say, does that star-spangled banner yet wave"
   e. "the mass of mankind has not been born with saddles on their back…"
   f. "[Andrew Jackson is] a barbarian and savage who can scarcely spell his own name. "

8. It is 1811, and you and your friends are called War Hawks. Write a broadside defending your position.

9. Thinking About the Big Ideas   Andrew Jackson was very different from any president before him. What factors contributed to his election? How did his election reflect changes in the nation's identity?

CHECK-UP 5

Answering the following questions will help you understand and remember what you have read in Chapters 21-23. Write your answers on a separate sheet of paper.

1. The United States entered the nineteenth century technologically backward. It left as the most modern nation in the world. Describe how each of the following people contributed to that transformation.
   a. Samuel Slater
   b. Eli Whitney
   c. Francis Cabot Lowell
   d. Robert Fulton
   e. Peter Cooper

2. Every region was changed by the Industrial Revolution, but differently. For each pair below describe how the region was affected by the technology.
   a. the North, mechanical looms
   b. the South, the cotton gin
   c. the West, modern transportation

3. It is 1840, and you are a reporter for a financial newspaper. Describe how the many new inventions are changing the American economy. Use the following terms.
   a. Industrial Revolution
   b. market revolution
   c. self-sufficient farm economy
   d. capitalist market economy

4. Americans often were referred to as "Yankees." Explain the phrase "Yankee Ingenuity" to a visitor from France.

5. Imagine you work in one of the mills in Pawtucket. Write a letter home describing your new life and compare it with life on the family farm.

6. Imagine you are Eli Whitney meeting with President John Adams and Vice President Thomas Jefferson. Explain why your factory-made muskets are better than the finest handcrafted ones.

7. Conduct an imaginary interview with Lucy Larcom. Decide what questions you would most like to have asked her, and write the responses you think she would have made.

8. What were some of the effects of the Erie Canal?

9. How would the railroad change America? Imagine that you are Charles Dickens predicting the future.

10. **Thinking About the Big Ideas**   Imagine what the United States would be like today if it had not industrialized. Write a short description that considers each of the following topics.
    a. wealth (Would the United States be one of the world's wealthiest nations?)
    b. population (Would so many immigrants have come to make a new life here?)
    c. cities (Would cities like New York have grown so large?)
    d. world power (Would the United States be a superpower?)

CHECK-UP 6

Answering the following questions will help you understand and remember what you have read in Chapters 24-30. Write your answers on a separate sheet of paper.

1. Write a question you would like to have asked each person below. Then write the responses you think each would have made.
   a. Sequoyah
   b. Andrew Jackson
   c. John Marshall
   d. Osceola
   e. Robert Carter III
   f. Eli Whitney

2. In the Jacksonian Era the frontier crossed the Mississippi. Western Georgia, Alabama, Texas, parts of Louisiana, and Florida became part of the new South. How were these places transformed? Consider the following questions.
   a. Who used to live there?
   b. How did they use the land?
   c. Who were the newcomers?
   d. How did the invention of the cotton gin help to transform the land?

3. Compare and contrast the strategies used by the Cherokee and the Seminole to save their homelands.

4. Define these terms and tell how they affected people's lives.
   a. "talking leaves"
   b. Trail of Tears
   c. homesteaders
   d. emancipated

5. There were many very different lifestyles in the South. Imagine that you are one of the people below. Describe a day in your life.
   a. yeoman farmer
   b. plantation owner
   c. slave

6. Imagine that you were with Daniel Boone when he returned to Kentucky after being away for 20 years. Write a diary entry describing your observations.

7. Imagine that you could interview François André Michaux. Decide what questions you would most like to have asked him and write the responses you think he would have made.

8. In what ways does the story of Robert Carter III illustrate the Age of Reason? Discuss in terms of the following.
   a. religion
   b. slavery

9. Summarize the intent of each of the following laws or legal cases.
   a. Indian Removal Act of 1830
   b. *Worcester* v. *Georgia*
   c. *Barron* v. *Baltimore*

10. **Thinking About the Big Ideas**   How do the lives of Andrew Jackson and Osceola reflect the changes taking place in the nation in this period?

CHECK-UP 7

Answering the following questions will help you understand and remember what you have read in Chapters 31-36. Write your answers on a separate sheet of paper.

1. The people listed below were champions of causes as well as being great orators or writers. Tell who each person was, and write something he might have said.
   a. William Lloyd Garrison
   b. Daniel Webster
   c. Henry Clay
   d. John C. Calhoun

2. Write one fact about each of the following presidents. It may be serious or humorous but it must be true.
   a. Martin Van Buren
   b. James Knox Polk
   c. James Buchanan

3. Explain the significance of each of these places in this period of our history.
   a. Missouri
   b. Maine
   c. Fort Ross

4. Define these terms and explain how each played a role in events of the period.
   a. abolition
   b. secession

5. In the first half of the nineteenth century, people's stands of important issues often depended on the geographic region in which they lived. Describe how and why people in the North and South differed on each of these issues.
   a. slavery
   b. states' rights
   c. tariffs

6. You are a recent immigrant. Decide in which region you will make your new home: the North, South, or West. Explain your choice.

7. Imagine that you could interview Frederick Douglass. Decide what questions you would most like to have asked him and write the responses you think he would have made.

8. Imagine you were in the Senate gallery for the great debate. Write a detailed description in a letter to a friend who lives out west.

9. Write an article for William Lloyd Garrison's newspaper using these terms.
   a. abolition
   b. moral
   c. immoral
   d. secession

10. **Thinking About the Big Ideas** Why did many Southerners feel that their way of life was threatened?

RESOURCE PAGE 1

Who Said It: Federalist or Democratic-Republican?

During Washington's presidency, many important issues had to be decided. Many focused on the federal government's power to raise revenue, promote manufacturing with protective tariffs, and create a federal bank. Disagreement about these gave rise to two parties, the Federalists (Hamilton's party) and the Democratic-Republicans (Jefferson's party).

Directions: Read the following quotations. Then use the information and what you already know to identify whether the statement was made by a Federalist or a Democratic-Republican. Write *F* or *D-R* on the line to show your choice.

1. About promoting manufacturing with protective tariffs:

_____ *Not only the wealth but the independence and security of a country appear to be…connected with the prosperity of manufactures.*

_____ *The political economists of Europe have established it as a principle that every state should endeavor to manufacture for itself.…In Europe…manufacture must…be resorted to of necessity…to support the surplus of their people. But we have an immensity of land courting the industry of the husbandman [farmer].…While we have land to labor, then, let us never wish to see our citizens occupied at a workbench [manufacturing].*

2. About banking:

_____ *I consider…that all powers not delegated to the United States by the Constitution, nor prohibited by it to the states, are reserved to the states, or to the people.…The incorporation of a bank,…[has] not, in my opinion, been delegated to the United States by the Constitution.*

3. About the federal government paying war debts of the states:

_____ *I…ask whether, if the war had been confined to a corner, instead of spreading over the Continent, and one State had incurred the whole debt of eighty millions, it would be just to leave the burden upon that State? Could it be called a state debt?*

_____ *Where…is the justice of compelling a state which has taxed her citizens for the sinking [repayment] of her debt, to pay…the debts of other states, which have made no exertions whatever?*

RESOURCE PAGE 2

The Census and the House of Representatives: 1790-1990

Directions: Use the text and chart below to find out more about how a census affects the House of Representatives.

The Constitution assigned a number of representatives for each state in the House of Representatives until the first census in 1790. The number of representatives was not to exceed one for every 30,000 people. (North Carolina and Rhode Island had not yet ratified the Constitution, and so did not send any representatives to the first Congress.)

In the 1900s, the ratio of people to representatives was changed. In 1920, the total number of members in the House was set at 435. As the population grows, each member of the House represents more people. In 1996, for example, approximately every 608,000 people had one representative.

STATE	NUMBER OF REPRESENTATIVES IN 1ST CONGRESS	POPULATION	NUMBER OF REPRESENTATIVES IN 107TH CONGRESS	POPULATION
Connecticut	5	237,655	5	3,287,116
Delaware	1	59,096	1	666,168
Georgia	3	82,548	11	6,478,216
Maryland	6	319,728	8	4,781,468
Massachusetts	8	378,556	10	6,016,425
New Hampshire	3	141,899	2	1,109,252
New Jersey	4	184,139	13	7,730,188
New York	6	340,241	30	17,990,455
North Carolina	0	395,005	12	6,628,637
Pennsylvania	8	433,611	18	11,881,643
Rhode Island	0	69,112	2	1,003,464
South Carolina	5	249,073	5	3,486,703
Virginia	10	747,550	8	6,187,358

RESOURCE PAGE 3

Foreign Policy Time Line, 1789-1809

Directions: Read about these important events in the foreign policy of the new nation. Write each event in the vertical bar on the time line that corresponds to the year in which it occurred. When you are finished, label the terms of the presidents in the horizontal bands on the time line. Then, on a separate sheet of paper, write a paragraph describing the effects of the major foreign policy decisions of Washington, Adams, or Jefferson.

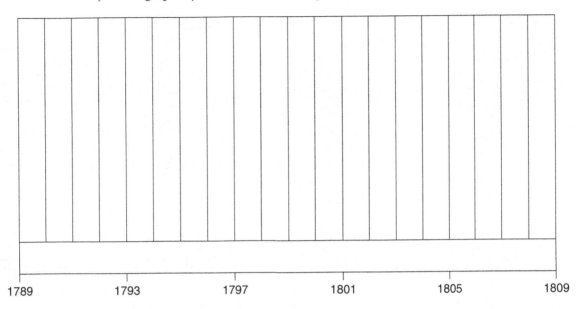

1789   1793   1797   1801   1805   1809

1793   **Neutrality Proclamation**—The President issues a declaration of neutrality in the war between France and England.

1794   **Jay Treaty**—This treaty with England resolves issues of debts, British forts in the Old Northwest, and the seizing of American sailors at sea.

1797   **XYZ Affair**—The president sends a commission to France to mend strained relations. Three French agents known as X, Y, and Z demand millions for France and thousands for themselves. Americans are outraged and mobilize for war.

1798   **Alien Acts**—The government gives itself the power to banish foreigners.

1800   **Treaty with Napoleon**—A treaty with Napoleon temporarily ends the threat of war with France.

1801   **Tripolitan War**—War is waged against the North African nation of Tripoli because of pirate attacks against American vessels.

1803   **Louisiana Purchase**—The president doubles the size of the nation by purchasing the Louisiana Territory from France.

1806   **Napoleonic Wars**—These European wars ruin much American commerce.

1807   **The Embargo Act**—Congress prohibits American ships from trading with foreign countries in retaliation for French and English laws preventing American ships from entering enemy harbors.

RESOURCE PAGE 4

Two Important Supreme Court Cases

Directions: First read about two cases that were brought before the Supreme Court in 1954 and 1969. Then read what the Constitution says about the subject. Finally, pretend that you are a Supreme Court justice. What judgment would you have handed down in each case? Write your decisions on a separate sheet of paper.

Brown v. Board of Education, Topeka, Kansas (1954)
Linda Brown, a student in the segregated Topeka, Kansas, school district, walked five miles to school each day. She was not allowed to attend a white school just across the train tracks from her home. Her father wanted her to attend the closest school possible. He sued the board of education, claiming that the segregated school system violated his daughter's constitutional rights.

What the Constitution Says
Article XIV. Section 1. All persons born or naturalized in the United States, and subject to the jurisdiction thereof, are citizens of the United States and of the state wherein they reside. No state shall make or enforce any law which shall abridge the privileges or immunities of citizens of the United States; nor shall any state deprive any person of life, liberty, or property without due process of law; nor deny to any person within its jurisdiction.

Tinker v. Des Moines (1969)
Some students and their parents in Des Moines, Iowa, organized a protest against the Vietnam War. Students planned to wear black armbands to school. When the school found out about the planned protest, they warned students and parents that they would suspend anyone who wore armbands. The children of the Tinker family were the only ones who wore their armbands to school, and they were suspended. Their parents sued the school district, saying it had violated the children's right of free speech. The school claimed that the armbands were disruptive.

What the Constitution Says
Article 1. Congress shall make no law respecting an establishment of religion or prohibiting the exercise thereof; or abridging the freedom of speech or of the press, or the right of the people peaceably to assemble and to petition the government for a redress of grievances.

Name _____ Date _____

RESOURCE PAGE 5

Eastern United States Relief Map

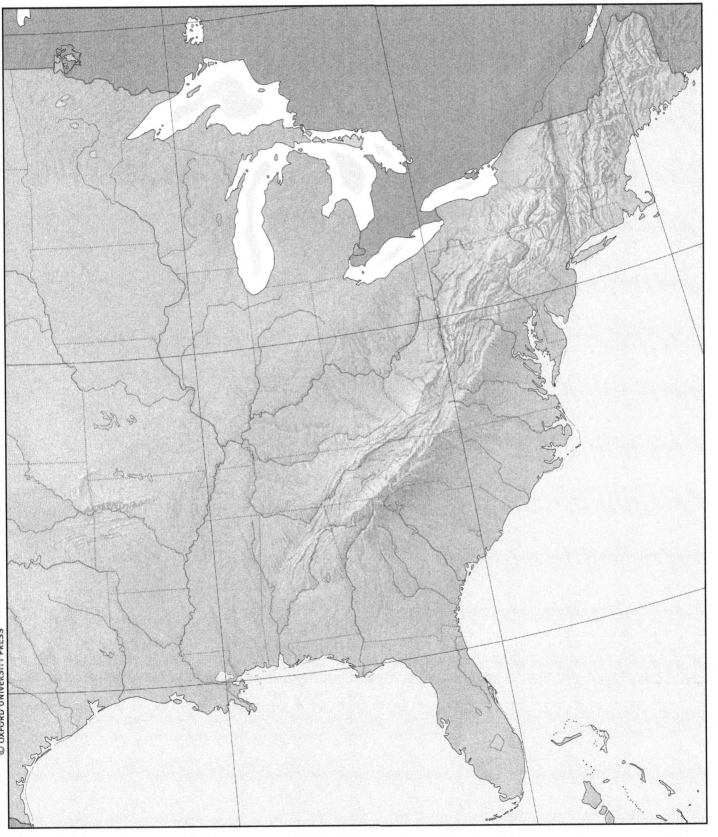

RESOURCE PAGE 6

The War of 1812: Causes and Effects

Although the Americans didn't win the War of 1812, they kept the British from winning it. This caused a feeling of greater national pride for Americans. Match other causes and effects of the War of 1812 by writing the letter of the effect on the line of the appropriate cause.

Causes

_____ 1. The British were busy at war with Napoleon until 1814.

_____ 2. The Federalists were opposed to the war.

_____ 3. Settlers in the West wanted to end British support of the Native Americans.

_____ 4. The British Navy set up a blockade of American ports.

_____ 5. Treaty of Ghent was signed on December 24, 1814.

_____ 6. After the war, the British withdrew from the West.

_____ 7. Imports of woolens, glass, and other goods manufactured in England stopped.

Effects

a. The war officially ended.

b. There was an increase in the manufacture of glass, woolens, and other goods in the United States.

c. Until 1814 most British forces were busy in Europe.

d. Native Americans in the West lost their most important ally.

e. The Federalists became known as unpatriotic.

f. Representatives from the West became War Hawks.

g. The economy of the United States was crippled and spiraled into a depression.

Use the information on this page and what you have already learned to write a paragraph describing the effects of the War of 1812.

_____

_____

_____

_____

_____

_____

_____

_____

RESOURCE PAGE 7

Foreign Policy Time Line, 1809-1825

Directions: Read about key developments in America's foreign policy. Write each event in the vertical bar on the time line that corresponds to the year in which the event occurred. When you are finished, label the terms of the presidents in the horizontal bands on the time line. Then write a paragraph on a separate sheet of paper that summarizes the foreign policy of one of the presidents on the time line.

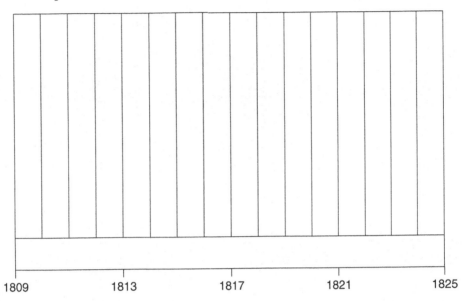

1809   1813   1817   1821   1825

1812   **War of 1812**—War is declared by Congress, and in the Campaign of 1812, the United States invades Canada unsuccessfully

1814   **Treaty of Ghent**—The United States and Great Britain end the conflict with no changes in territory.

1815   **Battle of New Orleans**—General Andrew Jackson defeats a British invasion at New Orleans. Neither side knows that the war is over.

1818   **Oregon Country**—The United States and Great Britain agree to joint occupation of Oregon Country.
        Florida Invasion—General Jackson invades and seizes Spanish Florida.

1821   **Florida Acquisition**—Spain agrees to give up Florida for $5 million.

1822   **Latin American Independence**—The United States recognizes the nations newly independent from Spain.

1823   **Monroe Doctrine**—President Monroe proclaims that no longer can any South or North American territory be colonized by European powers.

1824   **Protective Tariff**—Congress adopts the first protective tariff to help American manufacturing.

RESOURCE PAGE 8

The New Democrats and the 1828 Election

Directions: Use what you already know and the election map below to answer the questions.

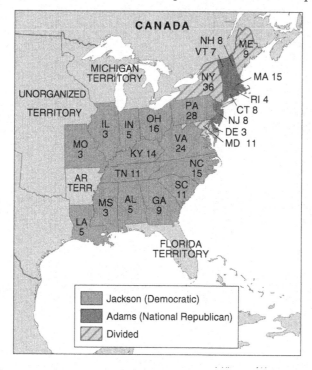

1. The Democratic party, won in 1828. What political leader did they rally around?

_____

2. The National Republican Party supported a strong federal government, a U.S. Bank, and high tariffs. Whom did they vote for in 1828?

_____

3. The Democrats stood for cheap land and low tariffs. What regions supported those principles?

_____

4. Which state had the largest number of electoral votes in 1828?

_____

5. Thomas Jefferson's Democratic-Republican Party was founded on confidence in the common man. Which party, Democratic or Republican, grew out of that tradition?

_____

6. Why didn't people in Florida, Michigan, and Arkansas vote in this election?

_____

RESOURCE PAGE 9

Cotton Production and Enslaved Population

Directions: Eli Whitney's invention of the cotton gin in 1793 dramatically changed the Southern economy. Use the data from the following tables to create two line graphs showing those changes. For each graph, add a title and labels for both axes. Then use your graphs to answer the questions that follow.

Southern Cotton Production, 1800–1860

Year	Bales
1800	100,000
1820	300,000
1840	1,350,000
1860	3,800,000

Southern Enslaved Population, 1800–1860

Year	Bales
1800	900,000
1820	1,500,000
1840	2,500,000
1860	4,000,000

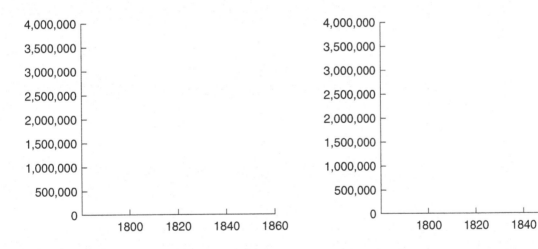

1. How does the trend in the enslaved population relate to the trend in cotton production?

_____

2. When was the sharpest increase in cotton production?

_____

3. In 1819, Florida joined the Union; in 1845, Texas joined the Union. How is the addition of these two states shown by the graphs?

_____

_____

RESOURCE PAGE 10

John Quincy Adams' Fourth of July Address, July 4, 1821 and The Monroe Doctrine (1823)

Directions: Read the passage below, taken from an address given to the House of Representatives by then-Secretary of State, John Quincy Adams. Then, answer the questions below.

"Wherever the standard of freedom and Independence has been or shall be unfurled, there will [America's] heart, her benedictions and her prayers be. But she goes not abroad, in search of monsters to destroy. She is the well-wisher to the freedom and independence of all. She is the champion and vindicator only of her own. She will commend the general cause by the countenance of her voice, and the benignant sympathy of her example. She well knows that by once enlisting under other banners than her own, were they even the banners of foreign independence, she would involve herself beyond the power of extrication, in all the wars of interest and intrigue, of individual avarice, envy, and ambition, which assume the colors and usurp the standard of freedom. The fundamental maxims of her policy would insensibly change from *liberty* to *force*. . . . She might become the dictatress of the world. She would be no longer the ruler of her own spirit. . . .

"[America's] glory is not *dominion*, but *liberty*. Her march is the march of the mind. She has a spear and a shield: but the motto upon her shield is, *Freedom, Independence, Peace*. This has been her Declaration: this has been, as far as her necessary intercourse with the rest of mankind would permit, her practice."

> benedictions- blessing
>
> vindicator- avenger
> countenance- composure
> benignant- kind
>
> extrication- liberation
> avarice- greed
> usurp- seize
> maxims- mottoes
> insensibly- heartlessly
>
> intercourse- interaction

At the time John Quincy Adams gave this speech to the House of Representatives, he was Secretary of State under President James Monroe. Two years later, President Monroe wrote *The Monroe Doctrine*. (You read about *The Monroe Doctrine* on p. 92. You can read the whole text in the Sourcebook.) Read the following passage from The Monroe Doctrine:

> Our policy, in regard to Europe . . . is, not to interfere in the internal concerns of any of its powers; to consider the government de facto as the legitimate government for us; to cultivate friendly relations with it, and to preserve those relations by a frank, firm, and manly policy, meeting, in all instances, the just claims of every power; submitting to injuries from none.

Would you say that John Quincy Adams agreed with The Monroe Doctrine? Find and underline two examples in his speech as evidence.

For discussion: Our official national policy on how our government interacts with foreign governments is what's meant by the phrase 'foreign policy.' You've probably heard that phrase before. Do you agree with John Quincy Adams? Should the foreign policy of the U.S. be to leave other countries alone and to keep out of their affairs? Why or why not? Give three good examples to support your position.

RESOURCE PAGE 11

Denmark Vesey

Directions: Read the following passage and discuss the questions below with your group.

After the execution of Denmark Vesey, an anonymously written tract was distributed, which contained the following observations on the conditions that allowed the uprising to occur:

"Previous to the proposal of any plan for preventing the recurrence of similar danger, it may be useful to advert to the causes which produced the late conspiracy. The following may be assigned as some of the most obvious: —1st, The example of St. Domingo, and (probably) the encouragement received from thence.—2dly, The indiscreet zeal in favor of universal liberty, expressed by many of our fellow-citizens in the States north and east of Maryland; aided by the Black population of those States.—3dly, The idleness, dissipation, and improper indulgencies permitted among all classes of the Negroes in Charleston, and particularly among the domestics: and, as the most dangerous of those indulgencies, their being taught to read and write: the first bringing the powerful operation of the Press to act on their uninformed and easily deluded minds; and the latter furnishing them with an instrument to carry into execution the mischievous suggestions of the former.—4th, The facility of obtaining money afforded by the nature of their occupations to those employed as mechanics, draymen, fishermen, butchers, porters, hucksters, &c.—5th, The disparity of numbers between the white and black inhabitants of the City. No effort of ours can remove some of these causes, but over others we may exercise control."

From "Reflections, Occasioned by the late Disturbances in Charleston."

St. Domingo-Slaves in Charleston would have known about this successful slave rebellion in Haiti.

dissipation-excess

indulgencies-indulgences

facility-ease
draymen-cartmen
disparity- imbalance

For group discussion:

Would you say that the author of this tract was for or against slavery?

Who are the "fellow-citizens" referred to in the second listed point?

Why would defenders of slavery consider teaching slaves to read and write as "the most dangerous of those indulgencies?"

What are the five causes the author gives that produced Denmark Vesey's rebellion?

Imagine that you are living in Charleston in 1822 and are planning a slave rebellion. Together with your group, discuss the five causes listed in the tract, and rank them in order of importance. Which is the most important in aiding a slave rebellion? Be prepared to present and defend your list to the class.

USING THE
MAP RESOURCE PAGES

These maps are black and white versions of the maps in the Atlas section of vol. 1, *The First Americans*, and vol. 4, *The New Nation*.

Exploring the West

Project suggestion: Use this map as reference or key for activities in vols. 4 & 5 that trace the routes of exploration in the West. The Lewis & Clark activity appears on TG page 44.

Native American Cultures

Project suggestion: Use this map in conjunction with activities that describe location and displacement of Native American nations. Locations of cultures on this map reflect the era before European settlement of the Western Hemisphere. These activities appear on TG pages 49 and 76.

These maps are provided for use with class projects and activities:

Reproducible US Relief Map*

Project suggestion: Use this map with the "Using Maps" activity described on TG page 26. Have students create a decade-by-decade overview of US territorial expansion as they read.

Alternately, use this map together with the Native Cultures Map for the "Map Project" activity described on TG page 49 (and the follow-up on TG page 76). Have students trace location and displacement of Native American peoples as they read.

Also, use this map for the "Geography Connections" activity described on TG page 58. Have students mark important battles and events in the War of 1812.

Reproducible Eastern US Relief Map*

Project suggestion: Use this map as an alternate for the "Map Project" activity described on TG page 49. Have students focus on eastern Native American peoples as they mark displacement caused by settlement and treaties.

Reproducible Western US Relief Map*

Project suggestion: Use this map together with the Exploring the West map for the "Geography Connections" activity described on TG page 44. Have students trace the exploration route of Lewis and Clark.

Reproducible Blank US Political Map w/ State Borders*

Project suggestion: Use this map with the "Using Maps" activity described on TG page 26. Have students create a decade-by-decade overview of US territorial expansion as they read.

Alternately, use this map with the "Analyzing Maps" activity described on TG page 26. Have students label and illustrate regional generalizations.

Reproducible US Political Comparison Map**

Project suggestion: Use this map with the "Using Maps" activity described on TG page 28. Have students sketch and compare the boundaries and regional demographics of the modern US and the US in 1790.

Also, in conjunction with this activity, use this map with the "Geography Connections" activity described on TG page 31 and follow-up on TG page 38. Have students mark locations for major US cities and population centers in 1790.

* These maps are also printed in each Student Study Guide for *The New Nation*.
** This map is printed in the Student Study Guide for *The New Nation* only.

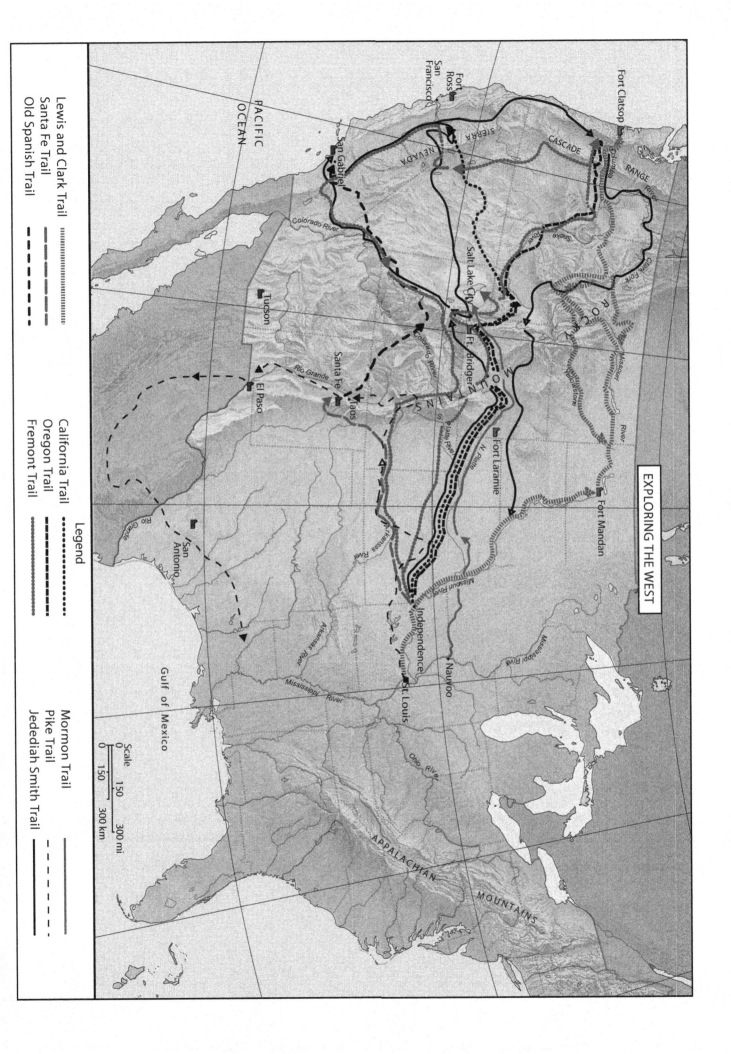

EXPLORING THE WEST

Legend

Lewis and Clark Trail
Santa Fe Trail
Old Spanish Trail

California Trail
Oregon Trail
Fremont Trail

Mormon Trail
Pike Trail
Jedediah Smith Trail

Scale
0   150   300 mi
0   150   300 km

PACIFIC OCEAN

Fort Ross
San Francisco
Fort Clatsop
San Gabriel
SIERRA NEVADA
CASCADE RANGE
Columbia River
Snake River
Clark Fork
Colorado River
Salt Lake City
Ft. Bridger
Tucson
Colorado River
Santa Fe
Taos
El Paso
Rio Grande
ROCKY MOUNTAINS
Missouri River
Yellowstone River
Fort Mandan
WASATCH MOUNTAINS
S. Platte River
N. Platte
Fort Laramie
Arkansas River
San Antonio
Rio Grande
Gulf of Mexico
Mississippi River
Arkansas River
Missouri River
Independence
St. Louis
Nauvoo
Ohio River
Mississippi River
APPALACHIAN MOUNTAINS

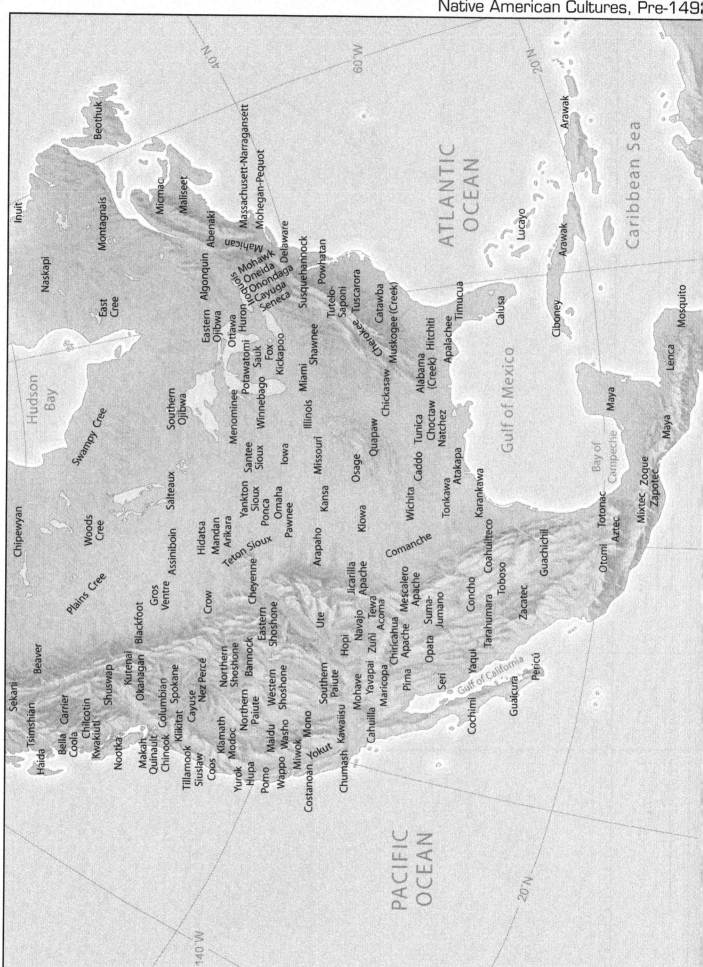

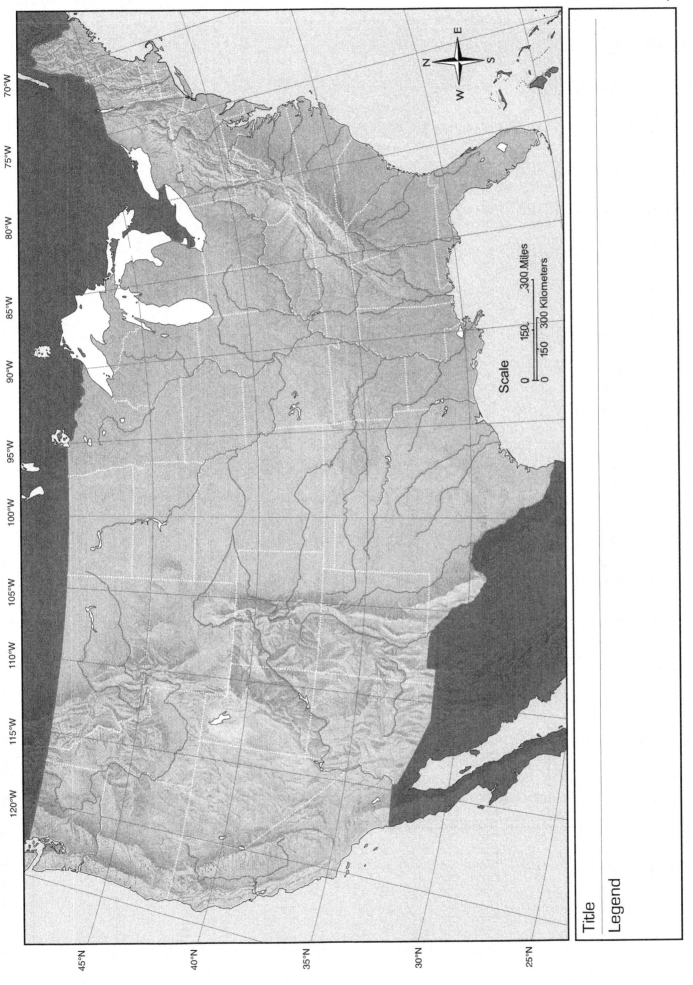

US Relief Map

Scale

300 Miles

150   300 Kilometers

150   300 Kilometers

0

0

70°W
75°W
80°W
85°W
90°W
95°W
100°W
105°W
110°W
115°W
120°W

45°N
40°N
35°N
30°N
25°N

N
E
S
W

Title

Legend

Scale

N
W   E
S

0   150   300 Miles

0   150   300 Kilometers

95°W   90°W   85°W   80°W   75°W   70°W

45°N

40°N

35°N

30°N

25°N

Title

Legend

Western US Relief Map

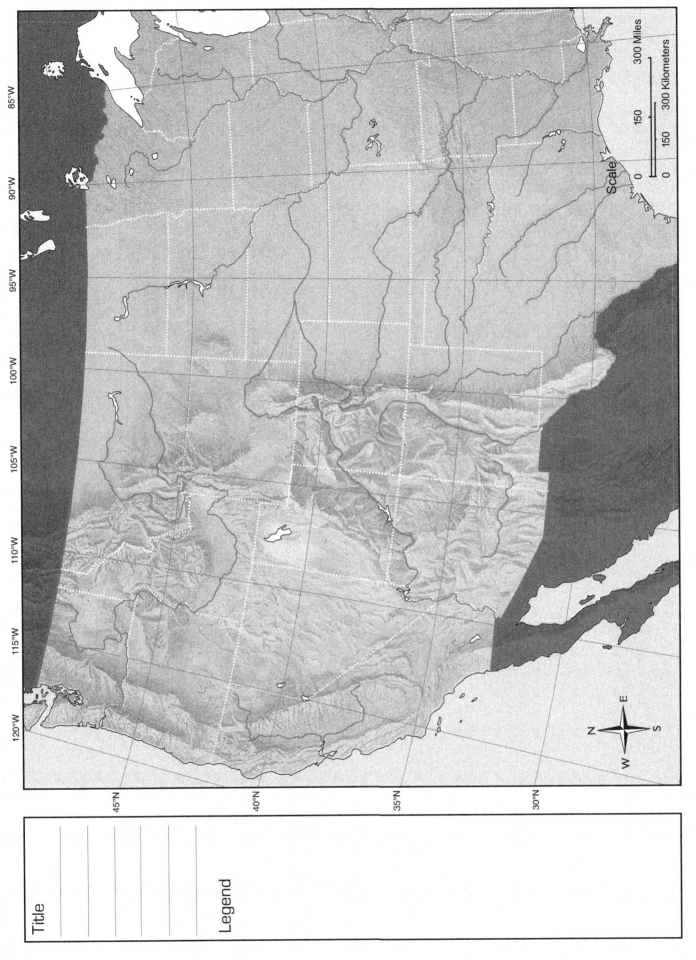

300 Miles

300 Kilometers

150

0

150

Scale

0

N

E

W

S

85°W

90°W

95°W

100°W

105°W

110°W

115°W

120°W

45°N

40°N

35°N

30°N

Title

Legend

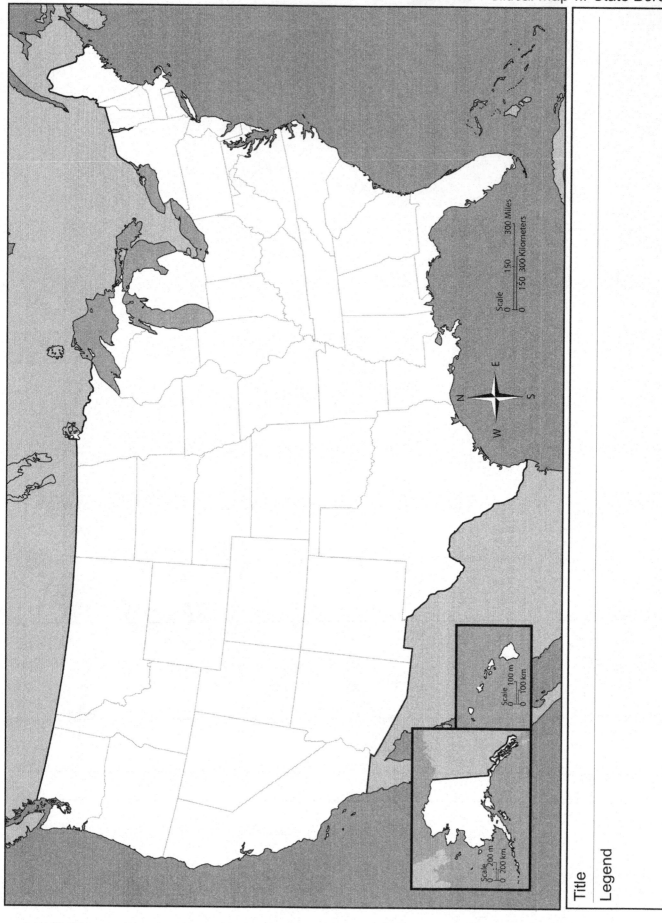

Scale
0   150   300 Miles
0   150 300 Kilometers

N E S W

Scale
0   100 m
0   100 km

Scale
0   200 m
0   200 km

Title

Legend

SCORING RUBRIC

The reproducibles on the following pages have been adapted from this rubric for use as handouts and a student self-scoring activity, with added focus on planning, cooperation, revision and presentation. You may wish to tailor the self-scoring activity—for example, asking students to comment on how low scores could be improved, or focusing only on specific rubric points. Use the Library/Media Center Research Log to help students focus and evaluate their research for projects and assignments.

As with any rubric, you should introduce and explain the rubric before students begin their assignments. The more thoroughly your students understand how they will be evaluated, the better prepared they will be to produce projects that fulfill your expectations.

	ORGANIZATION	CONTENT	ORAL/WRITTEN CONVENTIONS	GROUP PARTICIPATION
4	• Clearly addresses all parts of the writing task. • Demonstrates a clear understanding of purpose and audience. • Maintains a consistent point of view, focus, and organizational structure, including the effective use of transitions. • Includes a clearly presented central idea with relevant facts, details, and/or explanations.	• Demonstrates that the topic was well researched. • Uses only information that was essential and relevant to the topic. • Presents the topic thoroughly and accurately. • Reaches reasonable conclusions clearly based on evidence.	• Contains few, if any, errors in grammar, punctuation, capitalization, or spelling. • Uses a variety of sentence types. • Speaks clearly, using effective volume and intonation.	• Demonstrated high levels of participation and effective decision making. • Planned well and used time efficiently. • Demonstrated ability to negotiate opinions fairly and reach compromise when needed. • Utilized effective visual aids.
3	• Addresses all parts of the writing task. • Demonstrates a general understanding of purpose and audience. • Maintains a mostly consistent point of view, focus, and organizational structure, including the effective use of some transitions. • Presents a central idea with mostly relevant facts, details, and/or explanations.	• Demonstrates that the topic was sufficiently researched. • Uses mainly information that was essential and relevant to the topic. • Presents the topic accurately but leaves some aspects unexplored. • Reaches reasonable conclusions loosely related to evidence.	• Contains some errors in grammar, punctuation, capitalization, or spelling. • Uses a variety of sentence types. • Speaks somewhat clearly, using effective volume and intonation.	• Demonstrated good participation and decision making with few distractions. • Planning and used its time acceptably. • Demonstrated ability to negotiate opinions and compromise with little aggression or unfairness.
2	• Addresses only parts of the writing task. • Demonstrates little understanding of purpose and audience. • Maintains an inconsistent point of view, focus, and/or organizational structure, which may include ineffective or awkward transitions that do not unify important ideas. • Suggests a central idea with limited facts, details, and/or explanations.	• Demonstrates that the topic was minimally researched. • Uses a mix of relevant and irrelevant information. • Presents the topic with some factual errors and leaves some aspects unexplored. • Reaches conclusions that do not stem from evidence presented in the project.	• Contains several errors in grammar, punctuation, capitalization, or spelling. These errors may interfere with the reader's understanding of the writing. • Uses little variety in sentence types. • Speaks unclearly or too quickly. May interfere with the audience's understanding of the project.	• Demonstrated uneven participation or was often off-topic. Task distribution was lopsided. • Did not show a clear plan for the project, and did not use time well. • Allowed one or two opinions to dominate the activity, or had trouble reaching a fair consensus.
1	• Addresses only one part of the writing task. • Demonstrates no understanding of purpose and audience. • Lacks a point of view, focus, organizational structure, and transitions that unify important ideas. • Lacks a central idea but may contain marginally related facts, details, and/or explanations.	• Demonstrates that the topic was poorly researched. • Does not discriminate relevant from irrelevant information. • Presents the topic incompletely, with many factual errors. • Did not reach conclusions.	• Contains serious errors in grammar, punctuation, capitalization, or spelling. These errors interfere with the reader's understanding of the writing. • Uses no sentence variety. • Speaks unclearly. The audience must struggle to understand the project.	• Demonstrated poor participation by the majority of the group. Tasks were completed by a small minority. • Failed to show planning or effective use of time. • Was dominated by a single voice, or allowed hostility to derail the project.

NAME _____   **PROJECT** _____

DATE _____

ORGANIZATION & FOCUS	CONTENT	ORAL/WRITTEN CONVENTIONS	GROUP PARTICIPATION

COMMENTS AND SUGGESTIONS

UNDERSTANDING YOUR SCORE

Organization: Your project should be clear, focused on a main idea, and organized. You should use details and facts to support your main idea.

Content: You should use strong research skills. Your project should be thorough and accurate.

Oral/Written Conventions: For writing projects, you should use good composition, grammar, punctuation, and spelling, with a good variety of sentence types. For oral projects, you should engage the class using good public speaking skills.

Group Participation: Your group should cooperate fairly and use its time well to plan, assign and revise the tasks involved in the project.

_____

_____

_____

Use this worksheet to describe your project by finishing the sentences below.
For individual projects and writing assignments, use the "How I did" section.
For group projects, use both "How I did" and "How we did" sections.

The purpose of this project is to :

```
┌──────────────────────────────────────────────────────────────┐
│                                                              │
│                                                              │
│                                                              │
│                                                              │
└──────────────────────────────────────────────────────────────┘
```

Scoring Key =   **4** – extremely well
                3 – well
                2 – could have been better
                1 – not well at all

HOW I DID

I understood the purpose and requirements for this project…

I planned and organized my time and work…

This project showed clear organization that emphasized the central idea…

I supported my point with details and description…

I polished and revised this project…

I utilized correct grammar and good writing/speaking style…

Overall, this project met its purpose…

HOW WE DID

We divided up tasks…

We cooperated and listened to each other…

We talked through what we didn't understand…

We used all our time to make this project the best it could be…

Overall, as a group we worked together…

I contributed and cooperated with the team…

LIBRARY / MEDIA CENTER RESEARCH LOG

NAME _____

DUE DATE _____

What I Need to **Find**

Brainstorm: Other Sources and Places to Look

Places I **Know** to Look

I need to use:

☐ primary
☐ secondary
sources.

WHAT I FOUND

Title/Author/Location (call # or URL)

How I Found it

Rate each source
from 1 (low) to 4 (high)
in the categories below

Book/Periodical	Website	Other	Suggestion	Library Catalog	Browsing	Internet Search	Web link	Primary Source	Secondary Source	helpful	relevant
☐	☐	☐	☐	☐	☐	☐	☐	☐	☐	___	___
☐	☐	☐	☐	☐	☐	☐	☐	☐	☐	___	___
☐	☐	☐	☐	☐	☐	☐	☐	☐	☐	___	___
☐	☐	☐	☐	☐	☐	☐	☐	☐	☐	___	___
☐	☐	☐	☐	☐	☐	☐	☐	☐	☐	___	___
☐	☐	☐	☐	☐	☐	☐	☐	☐	☐	___	___
☐	☐	☐	☐	☐	☐	☐	☐	☐	☐	___	___

OUTLINE

MAIN IDEA: _____

_____

_____

    DETAIL: _____

_____

    DETAIL: _____

_____

    DETAIL: _____

_____

MAIN IDEA: _____

_____

_____

    DETAIL: _____

_____

    DETAIL: _____

_____

    DETAIL: _____

_____

Name _____ Date _____

MAIN IDEA MAP

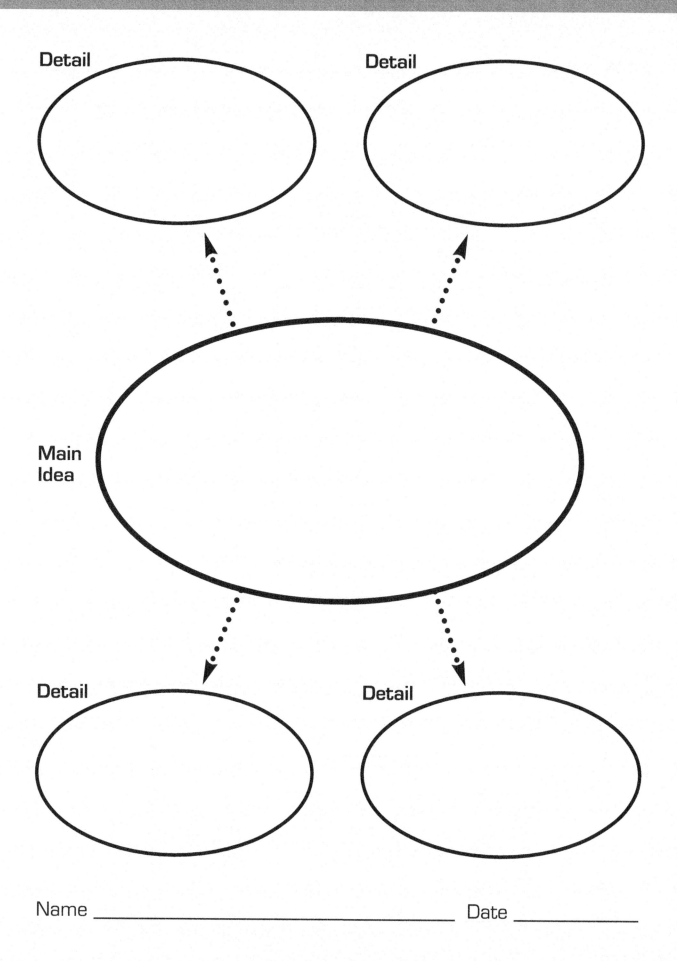

Detail

Detail

Main Idea

Detail

Detail

Name _____ Date _____

K-W-L CHART

K	W	L
What I Know	**What I Want to Know**	**What I Learned**

Name _____   Date _____

VENN DIAGRAM

Write differences in the circles. Write similarities where the circles overlap.

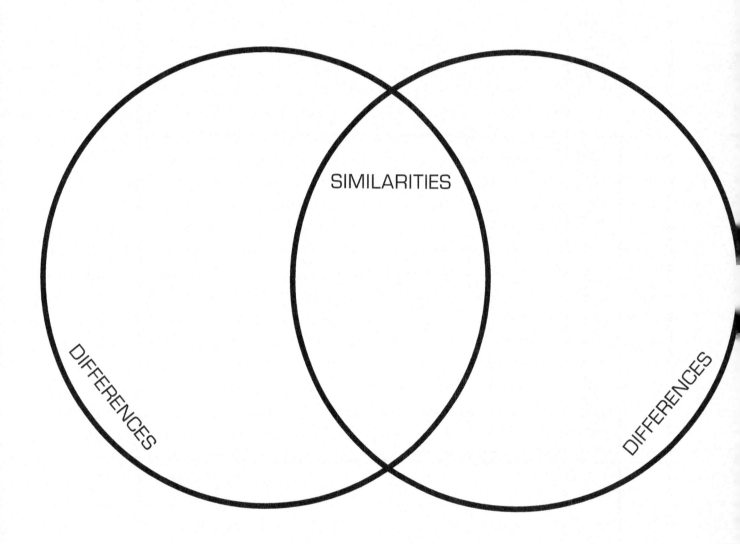

SIMILARITIES

DIFFERENCES

DIFFERENCES

Name _____ Date _____

TIMELINE

DATE

EVENT
Draw lines to connect the event to the correct year on the timeline.

Name _____ Date

SEQUENCE OF EVENTS CHART

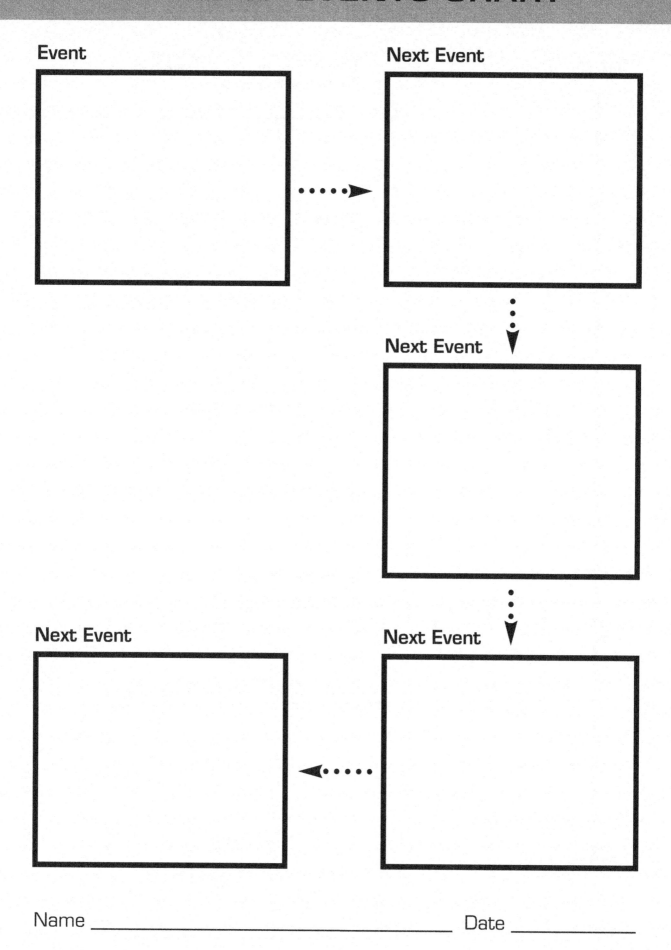

Event

Next Event

Next Event

Next Event

Next Event

Name _____ Date _____

T–CHART

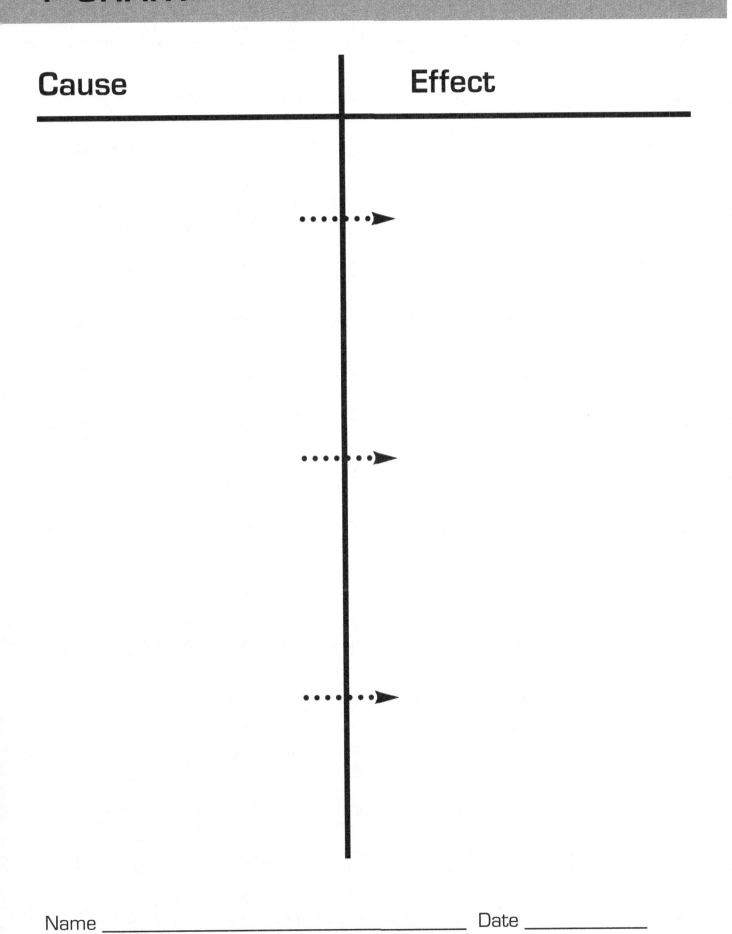

Cause | Effect

Name _____ Date _____

TEACHING GUIDE ANSWER KEY

CHECK-UP 1

1. (a) Jefferson and Hamilton were in Washington's cabinet. Jefferson held a liberal view of government and Hamilton a conservative view. (b) Banneker and L'Enfant worked on the plan for the Federal City. Banneker surveyed the land and L'Enfant was the designer. (c) Washington was elected the first president of the United States; Adams was elected the first vice president. 2. (a) The Mississippi River formed the western boundary of the United States in 1790. (b) The Potomac River was chosen as the site of the nation's capital because of its central location. (c) In 1790, nearly all U.S. citizens lived east of the Appalachians. The lands west of the mountains were mostly held by Native Americans. 3. (a) Conservatives—"tending to oppose change"; Hamilton. (b) Liberals—"favoring civil liberties, democratic reforms, and the use of government to promote social progress"; Jefferson. (c) Federalists—feared the masses and supported strong government led by educated aristocrats; Hamilton. (d) Republicans—feared strong government; Jefferson. 4. Responses should include some of these points: In a capitalist society (free-enterprise system), people who want to start a business usually begin with some capital and collateral. Then they can go to a bank or to investors and get credit. The collateral protects the investors in case the people default on the loan. Speculators take chances. 5. Responses should include some of the following points: (a) Many immigrants came for the cheap land, and with land they could support larger families. (b) With a healthy environment the birth rate was high and the death rate low. (c) Many people were leaving Europe where there were fewer opportunities. 6. Responses should include some of the following points: (a) A strong government led by educated aristocrats will protect liberty from the masses. (b) Strong government threatens the liberty of individuals and the states. (c) A strong government with good credit and a national bank could help business to grow. 7. Responses should include some of the following points: (a) A European monarch would be threatened. (b) Democracy would give hope to a European farmer with little land that he could improve his lot. (c) A European farmer with land might be threatened or hopeful. 8. It was the first free election in a modern democracy. The success of the republic influenced other people of other countries and led to other democratic revolutions. The process set in motion continues to this day.

CHECK-UP 2

1. (a) Adams was the 2nd U.S. president, Lyon was an outspoken congressman. Lyon: You are trying to act like a king. Adams: It's illegal to say those things about the president. (b) Jefferson was the 3rd U.S. president, Marshall was Chief Justice of the Supreme Court. Jefferson: Judicial review makes the courts too powerful. Marshall: Judicial review makes the constitution stronger and protects freedoms. (c) Hamilton was a Federalist, but when Burr ran for president, Hamilton supported Jefferson. Burr: How can you support Jefferson? Hamilton: Even though he is a Republican, he is a better man for the job. (d) Lewis and Clark explored the Louisiana Territory. Lewis: The President has asked me to form an expedition of exploration. Will you be my partner? Clark: Sure, that sounds great! (e) Ca-me-ah-wait was a chief of the Shoshone and Sacajawea was a Shoshone who helped Lewis and Clark. Sacajawea: My brother! My brother! It is I, Sacajawea! Ca-me-ah-wait: My long-lost sister, it is you! 2. Before the Purchase, the western border was the Mississippi River. After the Purchase, the Rocky Mountains formed the border between the Oregon Country and the United States. In the Southwest the nation was bordered by Mexico. (Students should note that the area of Mexico then was far larger than it is today). The Gulf of Mexico formed the southern border around New Orleans. 3. Responses should include some of the following points: (a) We came to a great rapids and had to take the boats from the river and portage miles before entering the water again. (b) We finally reached the source of the Missouri high in the mountains. (c) As we neared the mouth of the Columbia, we could hear the pounding surf of the Pacific Ocean. (d) Our hope to find a Northwest Passage died when we reached the great stone mountains. 4. The Sedition Act was unconstitutional because it abridged freedom of speech, which is guaranteed in the First Amendment to the Constitution. 5. It strengthened the judicial system, because it checked and balanced the executive and legislative branches. 6. (a) Federalists supported a strong central government; Republicans wanted as little government as possible. (b) Federalists supported England, and Republicans supported France. (c) Federalists supported the Alien and Sedition acts, and the Republicans opposed them. (d) Federalists did not like or support the French. Republicans admired the French. (e) Republicans proposed the Virginia and Kentucky Resolutions; Federalists opposed them. 7. Jefferson would say (a) The common man can govern himself. (b) Human nature needs to be set free. (c) The purpose of government is to protect life, liberty, and the pursuit of happiness. 8. Students might note that although the United States is a democracy, people without the right to vote were at the mercy of those with the vote unless their interests were the same. 9. Responses should include some of the following traits: independence, optimism, self-confidence, egalitarianism, democracy, belief in the common people.

CHECK-UP 3

1. (a) Red Jacket was a Seneca leader; Thomas Jefferson was U.S. president. Red Jacket: We have our own ways and our own religion and they are good ones. Jefferson: It would be better for your people to become like us or move far away from us to the west. (b) Tecumseh was a Shawnee leader; the Cherokee were a powerful nation that lived in the South. Tecumseh: We will all be overrun by the whites unless we unite and stop them. Cherokee Chiefs: The white people are not our enemy. We do not live the old way. (c) The Prophet was a Shawnee Medicine Man; William Harrison was governor of Indiana Territory. Prophet: This is our land and the Great Spirit will protect us. Harrison: Indiana Territory is being settled. It is no longer a place for Indians. (d) Osceola was a Red Stick Creek boy; Andrew Jackson was a U.S. general. Osceola: My people fought bravely but could not win and then you took our lands. Jackson: Your people sided with the British, now you lose everything. 2. (a) New York was already a state and the Iroquois had many new Americans for neighbors. (b) The frontier was quickly moving toward the Shawnee of Ohio. (c) The frontier was quickly moving toward the Creek of Alabama. 3. Factionalism nearly destroyed the Creek when, in the War of 1812, the two factions fought on opposite sides in a terrible civil war. Both sides lost. 4. In New York State there was a meeting held among the Seneca to hear a message from Christian ministers. The crowd was polite. Then their leader told the history of Indian/white relations. He respectfully said that for now the Indians would keep their ways until he saw that the white people's religion made their white neighbors good. 5. (a) many Iroquois; because they had fought with the British in the American Revolution (b) Red Sticks; because they lost all their lands after the Battle of Horseshoe Bend (c) Cherokee and White Sticks (d) Iroquois 6. (a) Jefferson hoped they would move west or learn to live as white people did. (b) The Shakers thought the Shawnee put the Christian world to shame. (c) Harrison thought that Indians endangered white settlers. 7. Responses should show an understanding of Tenskwatawa—a Shawnee medicine man who believed that returning to the old ways would give strength to all Native Americans and help them to resist white encroachment. 8. Responses should show an understanding of the fact that Native Americans had legal rights to their lands and that they did not want to move. 9. At the Battle of Tippecanoe, Tecumseh was killed and with him, his dream of a united Native American front died. At the Battle of Horseshoe Bend, the Red Sticks were defeated and lost their lands. Soon the White Sticks lost their lands, too. 10. Responses should recognize that the lives of all American Indians who came into contact with the New Americans were changed forever. Native Americans used every strategy available. They fled, resisted, adapted, attempted confederation, and fought back in an effort to preserve their land and identity.

CHECK-UP 4

1. (a) Perry was a captain in the U.S. Navy; Chauncey was an officer in the U.S. Navy. Perry: Why did you send me black men? I need good sailors. Chauncey: You will find these men as good as any men on board your vessel. (b) Ross was the British Major General who was sent to burn Washington, D.C. Madison was the First Lady. Ross: I see you have dinner here, madam. Thank you! Madison: You are welcome, but please sir, spare the house. (c) Pickersgill was the seamstress who made the flag for Fort McHenry. Key wrote the words to the "Star-

Spangled Banner." Key: So you are the seamstress who sewed the great flag that inspired us all. Pickersgill: Yes sir, and you are the poet who wrote the words that continue to inspire many. (d) Osceola was a military chief of the Seminole. Jackson had invaded Florida and became its governor. Osceola: You have pushed us to a place where nothing grows. The people are starving. Jackson: Your people will learn to live there. Northern Florida is for civilized settlers. (e) Royall was a newspaper reporter. Adams was U.S. president. Royall: Mr. President, I am here sitting on your clothes and will not leave until you answer my questions. Adams: Well, I do not give interviews but I guess I must this time. (f) Jefferson had been a Republican; Adams had been a Federalist. Jefferson: Long ago we argued about everything. Now we are old and friends, good friends. Adams: Yes, now I always look forward to your letters and do enjoy them so. 2. (a) The North had farms and villages. (b) The South had the most unequal distribution of wealth, a few mansions, and many very poor people. (c) The West was the frontier where people had a hard, independent lifestyle. 3. They both wanted the United States to gain territories: the War Hawks wanted Canada and Florida and the expansionists wanted the West. 4. Causes: British forts in the West, British support of Native Americans in the West, and British capture of American sailors. Results: a new sense of American pride for having defeated a superpower. 5. (a). Who does the American president think he is telling us what we can and cannot do? (b) We are important and powerful, and we can tell those European nations to keep their hands off our lands. (c) It is good that the United States recognizes our independence. 6. Responses should note Perry's prejudice against African-American sailors. 7. (a) Andrew Jackson (b) John Adams (c) Reverend John Gruber (d) Francis Scott Key (e) Thomas Jefferson (f) John Quincy Adams 8. Responses should include complaints about British support of Native Americans in the West, their presence in forts on American territory, and their taking American sailors at sea, and might include hawkish slogans such as, "We beat them once, let's finish the job!" 9. His military leadership in Florida and New Orleans, the growing influence of the West, the gradual acceptance of a government of the people–all these helped Jackson win. The victory of a man of the West, a man of the people, reflected new ideas about expansion, the changing geography of the United States as people moved west from the original states, and a changing population that had fewer ties to the colonial period.

CHECK-UP 5

1. (a). Slater brought the Industrial Revolution to America when he brought the plans (in his head) for a spinning mill. (b) Eli Whitney invented the cotton gin and the concept of interchangeable parts. (c) When Lowell returned from England, he brought the know-how for water-powered weaving and opened a weaving and spinning mill. (d) Fulton made a steam-powered riverboat. (e) Cooper made a steam powered railroad engine. 2. (a) Mechanical looms meant that people worked in factories for wages in the North instead of living on more self-sufficient farms. (b) The cotton gin meant that cotton could be grown profitably in a much greater area of the South and growers depended more on slave labor. (c) Modern transportation opened up the West to immigrants and enabled western farmers to send their goods east. 3. The Industrial Revolution is causing a market revolution because it is changing the nation's economy from a self-sufficient farm economy to a capitalist market economy. 4. Ingenuity means "inventiveness." Americans' knack for doing things for themselves made them confident and inventive. 5. Letters about mill life should note the long hours, low pay, poor working conditions, and/or new friends, new lifestyle, and wages. 6. Responses should note interchangeable parts. 7. Questions and answers should concern child labor. 8. Provided jobs for immigrants who were laborers; increased east-west trade and travel; encouraged people to spread west; helped towns and cities grow. 9. Responses should foresee the rapid movement of freight and people. 10. Responses should note that without industrialization, the nation would not be as wealthy or as populated, cities would not be the large centers of trade they are today, and the United States would not be a world power.

CHECK-UP 6

1. (a) Sequoyah desired to unite all Native American nations and stop the loss of Native American lands. (b) Andrew Jackson wanted all Native Americans to be removed west of the Mississippi. (c) In Worcester v. Georgia, Marshall said it was unconstitutional to push Indians off their lands. (d) Osceola, until his capture under a flag of truce, led the Seminole in their struggle to save their land. (e) Carter freed his slaves after a religious conversion. (f) Whitney's invention of the cotton gin sealed the fate of slaves in the South. 2. (a) Cherokee, Choctaw, Chickasaw, Creek, and Seminole (b) hunting, fishing, farms, orchards, some plantations (c) immigrants, settlers, or homesteaders (d) more land was cleared; forests were cut to grow cotton 3. The Cherokee went to Congress and used the courts to fight; the Seminole went to war. 4. (a) "Talking leaves" are what the Cherokee called their alphabet; the alphabet enabled the Cherokee to read and write in their own language. (b) The Trail of Tears was the forced journey west during the Indian removal. (c) Homesteaders were land-seeking settlers. The western lands they wanted were Indian lands. (d) Emancipated means "freed." It is what all enslaved people sought. 5. (a) Yeoman farmers worked their small farms usually without the help of any slaves. (b) Plantation owners lived at a leisurely pace. (c) Slaves, at the bottom of the ladder, worked the plantations and got little in return. 6. There are no longer the buffalo that roamed everywhere, and no deer that were once so plentiful, and few signs of bear. 7. Responses should reflect how Michaux was horrified at the American lack of concern for the environment. He was unhappy at the destruction of forests and the overgrazing that killed the native grasses. 8. During the Age of Reason, people were questioning the world. Robert Carter III questioned slavery and looked to religion for answers. 9. (a) made it legal for the president to move the tribes west (b) declared it unconstitutional to push Indians from their lands (c) allowed state laws to stand, even if they were unconstitutional 10. Jackson was a representative of a new class of Southerners who changed the way land was farmed and the way the nation was governed. He forced major changes on the American Indian population. Osceola's unsuccessful attempt to keep his world from being destroyed reflects the Indians' losing battle against change.

CHECK-UP 7

1. (a) Garrison was an abolitionist who published The Liberator in Massachusetts. (b) Webster was a congressman from Massachusetts who represented New England business interests and argued against states' rights and for Union. (c) Clay was a congressman from the West who was know as "the great compromiser," and who loved the Union. (d) Calhoun was vice president and represented the South. He argued for states' rights. 2. (a). Martin Van Buren or Old Kinderhook (O.K.) was the first president born a citizen of the U.S. He was president 8. (b) James Polk didn't like wasting time, dancing, or much music. Called the "hardest working man in the country," he was president 11. The U.S. got larger under Polk. (c) James Buchanan was president 15, but he didn't do much and Jackson called him an "old fool." 3. (a). In 1820, Missouri wanted to enter the Union as a slave state, which would upset the balance in Congress between slave and free states. (b) Maine was admitted to the Union as a free state in the Missouri Compromise to keep Congress balanced between slave and free states. (c) Fort Ross was a Russian fur trading post and community, developed in California. 4. (a). Abolition means "the ending or doing away with something, " so people who wanted to end slavery were called abolitionists. (b) The Southern states were talking of secession or withdrawing from the Union to protect what they claimed were their states' rights. 5. (a) In the agricultural South, many laborers were needed; therefore, slavery was considered economically necessary, and even a good or natural thing. Northern states had developed industries that didn't rely on slave labor; they outlawed slavery, and many Northerners were against it. (b) The South favored states' rights over federal laws in large part because federal laws could outlaw slavery. The North backed federal laws because a strong Union was to its advantage. (c) The industrial North favored tariffs, but the South called them an abomination and threatened to not collect them. 6. Most immigrants who could do so traveled to the West where land was available. People with less means stayed in the North where work was available. Few immigrants went South where most work was done by slaves and most land was taken. 7. Douglass was a former slave who realized that education was the key to freedom. He escaped to the North where he became a famous abolitionist, writer, and adviser to President Lincoln. 8. Hayne from South

Carolina urged the West to join the South to oppose the hated tariffs. He said that the government was formed by the states and they are the final power. Webster from Massachusetts argued that the government was made by the people and for the people and was answerable to the people, and that the Union has the final power. 9. Possible responses: The abolition of slavery is the only moral solution possible. Secession from the Union is an immoral solution because it would allow slavery to persist. 10. Abolitionists were growing in strength. The North was becoming more populous and thus more powerful in Congress. Northern interests were very different from Southern interests—for example, a tariff was passed that hurt the Southern economy. White Southerners believed that slavery was part of the identity of their region. Threats to slavery were literally and figuratively threats to Southern identity.

RESOURCE PAGE 1
1. F; D-R 2. D-R 3. F; D-R

RESOURCE PAGE 2
This Resource Page is to be used with Johns Hopkins Team Learning Activity on TG page 40.

RESOURCE PAGE 3
Students should place the events in the correct sequence on the time line. They should insert the following presidential terms: Washington 1789-1797; Adams 1797-1801; Jefferson 1801-1809.

RESOURCE PAGE 4
This Resource Page is to be used with Johns Hopkins Team Learning Activity on TG page 51.

RESOURCE PAGE 5
Students should use this map to indicate the Native Americans' land, as requested in the Teaching Guide for Part 3.
Answers for the Team Learning Activity on TG page 101 follow. Free states: Connecticut, Illinois, Indiana, Maine, Massachusetts, New Hampshire, New Jersey, New York, Ohio, Pennsylvania, Rhode Island, and Vermont; Slave states: Alabama, Delaware, Georgia, Kentucky, Louisiana, Maryland, Mississippi, Missouri, North Carolina, South Carolina, Tennessee, and Virginia. Students should draw the 36°30' parallel in the right place.

RESOURCE PAGE 6
1. c; 2. e; 3. f; 4. g; 5. a; 6. d; 7. b; paragraphs will vary

RESOURCE PAGE 7
Students should place the events in the correct sequence on the time line and label the following presidential terms: Madison 1809-1817; Monroe 1817-1825.

RESOURCE PAGE 8
1. Andrew Jackson 2. John Quincy Adams 3. the South and the West (as well as some of the North) 4. New York 5. the Democratic Party 6. Florida, Michigan, and Arkansas were territories, so their citizens could not vote in national elections.

RESOURCE PAGE 9
Students should title and label their line graphs correctly. 1. Both kept increasing, slowly at first and then more and more dramatically. 2. between 1840 and 1860 3. Increases in both cotton production and the enslaved population after those dates show the impact admission of these two states had on the economy of the South.

STUDENT STUDY GUIDE
ANSWER KEY:
Answers for writing prompts and open-ended activities are not included in this key.

CHAPTER 1
Word Bank 1. monarchy 2. president elect 3. tsars 4. inauguration
Writing humble

CHAPTER 2
Word Bank 1. judicial 2. dictatorship 3. executive 4. cabinet 5. legislative
Primary Source 1. interested and moved 2. captivated and excited

CHAPTER 3
Word Bank 1. Democratic-Republican 2. interest 3. free enterprise system 4. liberal 5. Federalist 6. collateral 7. bond 8. invest 9. conservative 10. credit 11. capital; *similar meanings:* capitalist & free enterprise system. *opposite meanings:* liberal & conservative
Critical Thinking *Hamilton:* feared the masses; wanted the government to pay off its debt; encouraged business and industry; wanted aristocratic leaders to govern. *Jefferson:* wanted a free education amendment; had faith in ordinary people; feared a powerful government; fought for freedom of the press. *Both:* concerned about balancing liberty and power; headed a major political party.
Primary Source 1. Alexander Hamilton. 2. *He could handle the Nation's dollars.; And he yoked the States together.*

CHAPTER 4
Word Bank capital; Capitol
Comprehension 1. Ellicott surveyed the land for the city. 2. Banneker assisted Ellicott. 3. L'Enfant planned the city and designed several buildings. 4. Hoban was the architect of the White House. 5. Thornton designed the Capitol.
George Washington and Thomas Jefferson

CHAPTER 5
Word Bank 1. inhabitants
Map 1. Virginia 2. 750,000 3. Kentucky, Georgia, and Delaware
Primary Source 1. The assessment could be interpreted as positive or negative. 2. He describes it as a backwoods and wild.

CHAPTER 6
Word Bank 1. Executive Mansion 2. Oval Office
Critical Thinking *valid inferences:* The buildings were newly built; It could be reached by boat; The members of Congress had been to the city.
Primary Source 1. the size of the house; the oval room in the house; the house's potential 2. the lack of bells in the house; the house being unfinished; no fences.

CHAPTER 7
Word Bank 1. diplomat; protocol
Critical Thinking 1. opinion 2. fact 3. fact 4. opinion 5. opinion 6. fact 7. opinion 8. fact

CHAPTER 8
Word Bank 1. checks and balances 2. Alien and Sedition Acts 3. excises
Primary Source 1. Congress 2. worship; peaceable assembly; petitioning the government

CHAPTER 9
Timeline 1798 – Congress passes the Alien and Sedition Acts. 1799 – John Marshall is elected to Congress. 1800 – Election ends in a tie between Jefferson and Burr. 1803 – Marbury v. Madison decision 1804 – 12th amendment
Primary Source 1. pure; broadminded; good temper; unwearied patience 2. detested Thomas Jefferson 3. student answers will vary

CHAPTER 10
Word Bank 1. protective tariff
Critical Thinking 4, 6, 1, 5, 2, 3
Primary Source 1. The country should be united. 2. Student answers will vary.

CHAPTER 11

Word Bank 1. "a water route across North America" 2. sentences will vary 3. sentences will vary

Map *Lewis and Clark route appears on SE pp 60-61.* 1. St. Louis 2. Missouri River and Columbia River 3. To indicate the Louisiana Purchase area 4. Pacific Ocean

Primary Source 1. soil; vegetable growth; animals; mineral productions; volcanic occurances 2. written on paper of the birch tree 3. possible answers: laptop computer; tape recorder; digital camera

CHAPTER 12

Word Bank 1. orator 2. incorporate

Critical Thinking *valid inferences:* The Christian missionaries believed their religion was superior to that of the Iroquois; The earliest white settlers of North America relied upon the Indians for help; Religion was important to the Iroquois.

Primary Source 1. They welcomed the settlers as friends. 2. The settlers wanted the Indians' land. 3. The settlers grew in number and brought strong liquor to the Indians.

Writing worried

CHAPTER 13

Word Bank 1. Shakers

Map 1. present-day Ohio 2. Tecumseh's journeys 3. Florida 4. British

Critical Thinking *Tekamthi:* born under a shooting star; a great warrior; muscular and handsome; his name means "The Panther Passing Across." *Tenskwatawa:* also called "The Prophet"; a shaman; defeated at Tippecanoe. *Both:* wanted Indians to be proud of their heritage; fought against the Americans in battle ; a Shawnee leader.

CHAPTER 14

Word Bank 1. Red Sticks 2. White Sticks

Comprehension 1. Alabama, Georgia, and Carolina 2. Florida 3. Florida

CHAPTER 15

Word Bank 1.anthem 2. John Bull 3. War Hawks

Map *1812 map appears on SE p. 77.* 1. British 2. Indian forces 3. five 4. The British blockade 5. Canada.

Primary Source 1. The American flag 2. It is sung at modern sporting events.

CHAPTER 16

Word Bank corsairs; Barbary States; bey

Timeline 1797 – built. 1804 – shelled Tripoli. 1812 – defeated the Guerrière and received the name "Old Ironsides." 1830 – Oliver Wendell Holmes wrote a poem to save the ship. 1844 – embarked on a round-the-world voyage. 1897 – moved to Boston on 100th birthday. 1997 – sailed into Boston harbor on 200th birthday.

Primary Source 1. admiration. 2. Officials were planning to scrap the ship. 3. sinking out at sea.

CHAPTER 17

Word Bank 1. expansionist 2. Monroe Doctrine

Critical Thinking 1. before 2. before 3. after 4. after 5. after 6. after

CHAPTER 18

With a Parent or Partner ambassador; envoy; representative negotiator

Primary Source 1. covered with shrub-oaks and uninhabited 2. Thomas Jefferson 3. No cell phones; possible to visit an ex-president without security clearance; tobacco barrels rolled to market

CHAPTER 19

Access John Quincy Adams

Comprehension 1. to celebrate the 50th anniversary of the signing of the Declaration of Independence 2. Quincy, Massachusetts 3. Monticello, Virginia 4. They were old and ailing.

Primary Source 1. a duration of time from which succeeding years are reckoned 2. abuse of political institutions 3. use their minds for the good of America

CHAPTER 20

Word Bank 1. Old Hickory 2. spoils system

Timeline 1767 – born in a log cabin. 1780 – joins the South Carolina militia. 1788 – appointed attorney general for the Tennessee region. 1815 – led troops to victory at the Battle of New Orleans. 1829 – inaugurated president of the United States. 1833 – becomes the first U.S. president to ride on a train.

Critical Thinking 1. fact 2. fact 3. opinion 4. opinion 5. fact 6. opinion 7. fact 8. opinion

CHAPTER 21

Word Bank Industrial Revolution; cotton gin; interchangeable parts; market revolution; farm economy; market economy

Primary Source 1. She probably would have welcomed the growth of factories. 2. She was not happy—she missed school. 3. Students should base their responses on their answers to questions 1 & 2.

CHAPTER 22

Word Bank 1. celeripede 2. macadam 3. pike 4. corduroy

Critical Thinking 4, 6, 1, 3, 2, 5

Primary Source 1. a thin layer of broken stones 2. poorly constructed 3. stone bridges

CHAPTER 23

Word Bank 1. locomotives 2. iron horses 3. steam power

Map 1. 1840 2. roads and trails 3. north and east 4. a canal 5. Spanish territory

Critical Thinking Steamboats: Robert Fulton was an important inventor; the North River was an early example, traveled up the Mississippi River. Railroads: could travel at 30 miles per hour, George Stephenson was an important inventor, Baltimore & Ohio, relied on tracks, first appeared in England. Both: relied on steam power; changed transportation in America

Primary Source 1. happiness; joy 2. student answers will vary 3. down the Ohio River

CHAPTER 24

Word Bank 1. The law that made it legal for the president to move Indian tribes west. 2. The removal of the Indians from the Southeast was a dark period in U.S. history.

Map 1. 1825-1850 2. Cherokee 3. move west to Indian Territory 4. Oklahoma and Kansas; could also list Nebraska

Critical Thinking Valid Conclusions: 1, 4, 5, 7

Primary Source 1. Yes. The language he created was an important advance for the Cherokee. 2. Yes. White men

CHAPTER 25

Timeline 1831 - John Marshall rules in the Barron v. Baltimore case; The Choctaws are forced to move west. 1832 - Black Hawk leads a campaign to regain the Sauk and Fox homelands; Henry Clay runs for president against Andrew Jackson. 1834 - The Chickasaws are forced to move west. 1836 - The Creeks are forced to move west. 1838 - The Cherokees are forced to move west.

Comprehension 1. minister 2. license to preach 3. John Marshall 4. Worcester and the Indians 5. He ignored it.

CHAPTER 26

Word Bank 1. guerilla bands 2. Homesteaders

Critical Thinking 1. d 2. c 3. a 4. f 5. b 6. e

Primary Source 1. They hated the idea. 2. They believed they could not live alongside white people. 3. Student answers will vary.

CHAPTER 27

Word Bank 1. bigotry 2. hypocrisy

Critical Thinking a slave is sold and separated from his wife; a white person is arrested in 1810 for importing a slave from Africa; a black person owns slaves; a master abuses a slave; a child becomes a slave at birth; a white person calls for the end of slavery; white people hunt for a runaway slave

Primary Source 1. white people 2. The idea is absurd and violates reason. 3. The writer wants equal rights for black people, and slavery to end.

CHAPTER 28

Word Bank 1. established church 2. Age of Reason 3. dissenting church 4. emancipated

Critical Thinking *Robert Carter III:* lived in a home called Nomini Hall; supported the Virginia Statue for Religious Freedom; freed his

slaves; became a deist, and then a Baptist; grandson of "King Robin" *Henry Laurens:* the wealthiest merchant in Charleston; member of the Continental Congress; imprisoned in the Tower of London both; owned many slaves; believed slavery was wrong;
Primary Source 1. Slavery is immoral and unjust. 2. Answers will vary.

CHAPTER 29
Word Bank 1. pastor 2. auction 3. oppressions
Critical Thinking *Free Blacks:* Richard Allen; Paul Cuffe; Quock Walker; Elizabeth Freeman; Josiah Henson; George R. Allen. *Slaves:* Richard Allen; Quock Walker; Elizabeth Freeman; Josiah Henson; Moses Grandy. *Whites:* Lafayette; James Madison; John Woolman
Primary Source 1. It tore families apart. 2. They hated it. 3. Student answers will vary.

CHAPTER 30
Word Bank 1. coffle 2. yeoman farmers 3. lynch
Comprehension 1. 300 2. Article 1, Section 9 3. tell stories 4. John C. Calhoun & Jefferson Davis 5. Cotton brought great wealth to the South.
Primary Source 1. Slave owners 2. Student answers will vary.

CHAPTER 31
Word Bank 1. secede 2. Missouri Compromise 3. abolition
Critical Thinking 1. fact 2. opinion 3. opinion 4. fact 5. fact 6. opinion 7. fact 8. opinion
Primary Source 1. Both took part in a rebellion to win freedoms. 2. Answers will vary.

CHAPTER 32
Word Bank 1. Slave catchers 2. freeman
Map *For map activity use territories as marked in Book 6 atlas section, "Free States and Slave States"* 1. the first 13 states 2. Pittsburgh, Cincinnati, and Cairo 3. Andrew Jackson 4. Iowa, Minnesota, and Wisconsin 5. Missouri
Critical Thinking 3, 1, 4, 6, 5, 2
Primary Source 1. white people 2. black people 3. White people limited the opportunities of black people and then criticized black people for not achieving more.

CHAPTER 33
Word Bank Free Soil Party
Critical Thinking *Van Buren:* first president born a U.S. citizen; replaced Andrew Jackson. *Harrison:* president for only 31 days; Old Tippecanoe. *Tyler:* referred to as "His Accidency;" Whigs kicked him out of their party. *Polk:* "I am the hardest working man in the country;" died of exhaustion three months after his term. *Taylor:* "Old Rough and Ready;" second president to die in office. *Fillmore:* sent Commodore Matthew Perry to Japan; installed first kitchen stove in the White House. *Pierce:* graduated from Bowdoin College; from New Hampshire. *Buchanan:* the only bachelor president; succeeded by Abraham Lincoln.
Primary Source 1. James Buchanan 2. The best person does not always get the job. 3. They were not considered as important as they are today.

CHAPTER 34
Word Bank 1. tariff 2. oratory 3. Whig 4. triumvirate
Critical Thinking *Clay:* U.S. senator; wanted to be president; known as "the great compromiser"; spoke out against slavery; represented a slave state; a powerful speaker; speaker of the House of Representatives. *Webster:* U.S. senator; supported Massachusetts shipowners; wanted to be president; spoke out against slavery; a powerful speaker; a Yankee. *Calhoun:* U.S. Senator; wanted to be president; defended the Southern way of life; represented a slave state; Andrew Jackson's vice president; a powerful speaker; opposed the collection of tariffs.
Primary Source 1. John C. Calhoun 2. slavery is necessary in advanced societies 3. student answers will vary

CHAPTER 35
Word Bank 1. secession 2. sovereign; sovereign
Critical Thinking 1. opinion 2. fact 3. fact 4. opinion 5. opinion 6. opinion 7. fact 8. fact
Primary Source 1. It is a right that all people are born with. 2. peaceful protests; petitions; voting; speeches

CHAPTER 36
Comprehension 1. Illinois 2. First he supported it; then he opposed its spread; finally he saw it as evil. 3. women
Primary Source 1. Jackson believed that both whites and blacks could gain eternal life. 2. Yes, he owned slaves and promoted the rights of white people only.